Jill Stephens began writing when she retired from full-time work. Her first self-published work was a series of illustrated short stories entitled *Tales of the Malmesbury Merrie Monks*. This proved popular locally, but she was unable to promote them when she became a carer for her very elderly mother. Further tales were not formally published but some were enjoyed, even on local radio.

Cruel Mistress was started by way of showing her children that there was a reason for their father's behaviour, and that he was at heart a good man. Writing the book was cathartic, and she remembered the happy times and never really gave up on him over the fifty years they were together.

The combination of life in the navy with its drinking culture, not admitting to problems and then the trauma of war takes its toll. She is glad that now there is a greater recognition of post-traumatic stress and the problems not only faced by members of the armed forces but also their families. For this reason, she hopes that her own tale will reach out and help others to seek help before more damage is done to both health and relationships.

Since writing this autobiography, she has written novels and more short stories and enjoys membership of a writing group in her hometown.

To members of the armed forces and emergency services whose experiences we cannot share, but we see the effects written on your lives and those of your families. Also, to the Royal British Legion and others who try to put those lives back together.

Jill Stephens

CRUEL MISTRESS

THE WIFE'S TALE

AUSTIN MACAULEY PUBLISHERS™

LONDON • CAMBRIDGE • NEW YORK • SHARJAH

A CIP catalogue record for this title is available from the British Library.

ISBN 9781528912754 (Paperback)
ISBN 9781528960243 (ePub e-book)

www.austinmacauley.com

First Published (2019)
Austin Macauley Publishers Ltd
25 Canada Square
Canary Wharf
London
E14 5LQ

Introduction

I suppose I should have known better than to go and live in Gosport. My father was a sailor, and I had grown up watching the way that he changed when he had had one too many.

My mother was of the generation of obedient wives who accepted their lot on the basis that after marriage they would keep house, and their husband would be the breadwinner. She was obviously not happy the way things were much of the time, but had no great urge to live otherwise. How desperately unhappy she was, I only came to know later when I went on holiday with her for two weeks after she had nursed my father through hepatitis, and he had finally forsworn drinking.

I was of more independent nature and had a career or two, so I was determined that my life would not be made the misery that hers was.

To what extent I was successful, you will find in this book.

Names have been changed, and I dedicate this book to my family whose love and whose needs sustained me in difficult times.

My thanks too to all those friends who listened when I needed to talk and helped when I needed extra hands.

Jill Stephens
2017

Cruel Mistress
(The Wife's Tale)

Whom does he see
As he looks in the glass?
How attractive is she
That she can surpass
The love that we had for each other?

Whoever she is
Whatever she gives
It is not just the fizz
Of pleasure that lives
In the way that they cling to each other.

For gloom fills his face
And his heart is sad
"Keep out" is writ large
And his thoughts must be bad
For we cannot reach one another.

Scarce does he come home
As the clock ticks the hour
To her arms he has flown
And the evening turns sour
They can't get enough of each other.

A woman could I fight
But in a bottle or in can
This mistress has no right
To lay hold of my man.
Fight the one, but how counter the other?

I can't reach him now
As he sits there in gloom
A frown creases his brow
And I leave the room
For now we are lost to each other

I stamp, rail and shout
But I can't bring him back
And then I walk out
Get myself off the rack
For we are destroying each other.

The children have left
I stayed there 'til then
But I feel bereft
And I've no faith in men.
Are they all just as bad as each other?

Or was it my fault?
Did I not fight enough?
Should I have called halt
Before life was so rough.
I thought we were there for each other.

His mistress has him in thrall
In her private hell
For her he gives all
And his soul he would sell
To get more and more of the other.

Now see how she knows
Her superior strength
They come not to blows
But he stretches his length
Enslaved and abused by the other.

His health in decline
He goes down the slope
He steps over the line
To the land of no hope
Unreachable there, with the other.

And now I feel old
And he's broken in health.
Still loves me, I'm told
But she's taken by stealth
Our youth and our future together.

I no longer feel cross
But the hurt has gone deep
I grieve for my loss
And often I weep
For the waste of the life of the other.

Loving father and best friend
Strong support, safe provider
She has brought him at the end
Shambling, broken, an outsider
Friendless, lonely, shamed, and yet
Deep inside, the man is still
Hidden, waiting there 'til
His future finally is set.

He'll shake her off, return to life
Or p'raps in death will find release.
Think then of me, who was his wife
Wondering how that life will cease.

Written in 2003

Chapter One
What Did He See in the Glass?

"Speak to me! Tell me! Don't turn away!"

It was a silent scream.

Frustration boiled over and she gripped the plate she was drying. You hear of people throwing things. It would be very easy.

The plate slipped through her fingers and smashed to bits on the stone floor. Now she had something to focus on, and she was able to swear, "Damn, Damn, Damn!"

She bent down to pick up the pieces. Her husband turned back full of concern and hurried to get the dustpan and brush. He had no idea how close he had come to being on the receiving end of a discus.

'Men! They have no idea how much they can wind you up just by hiding their feelings. This stiff upper lip business is such a nonsense. They keep things bottled up so tightly that at some point you just knew that something had to blow in either him or you. He prided himself in not losing his temper. The same couldn't always be said for me, though it was mainly verbal and quickly over. Better that than going into a sulk or a shell or whatever it was.

'This business of going down to the pub as soon as it opened didn't help things. The neighbours could set their clocks by him. It wasn't a social thing. Maybe he would have a few words with the barmaid but he had no real friends down there. He didn't have many friends at all come to think of it. He got on well with the people he worked with, but they were ships that passed in the night. Ships, that was what it was all about in the Navy. You spend time with each other then you are moved on in different directions. Unless you have friends from your school days you are pretty much a rolling stone.

'Anyway, he would go down to the pub sober and come back if not drunk, then the worse for wear and miserable with it. It was just a way to get several drinks inside him to dull his senses and turn him into such a moody and miserable fellow that he was certainly not the man he used to be.

'I really don't like this new man. The kids avoid him and even the dogs have their tails between their legs when he comes back from the pub. Though, they are all over him when he comes back from work and takes them out for a walk.

'Underneath he is still a nice man, thoughtful, loving even. It just that shell, that carapace, that armour that he has had ever since he got back from the war. He is drinking to forget something, but I don't know what. I'm sure he could get help if only he would open up, but he won't. The gulf gets wider between him and me and between him and those he really loves – his children. This is perhaps what hurts me more than anything else.

'The dogs still get some affection because they demand it but the rest of us have to walk on eggshells. I mutter "Blessed are the peacemakers" as he goes out of the door and takes his bottle of homemade wine and his tumbler to the stump. He will be there now until it is dark and he stumbles in and up to bed and snores. How he snores! The walls vibrate.

'At least, the girls and I can watch what we like on the television and have a bit of partial family time on a dry night. When it is raining, he sits in his chair, a dog on either side and the girls go upstairs to their record-players until it is bed-time and I retreat to the dining room to get on with some marking. We are no longer a family, just a group of individuals in a house.

'Is this what marriage is all about and where did it all go wrong?

'I thought we had had all our troubles at the start and now that the girls are older we would become closer.

'Wrong! God knows I have had enough times of being lonely.

'They call it the marriage trap and that is what it could become. If your husband isn't there, you are neither fish nor fowl. You can't go out and dance the night away as if you were still single (mind you, I probably had more time as a wallflower than dancing, as I was taller than most of my girlfriends and being an only child I had not had so much opportunity to learn social chit-chat or be the life and soul of the party). You are not exactly the first on the list to be invited to a dinner-party either. You have got out of the habit of going out with your girlfriends, especially, if you have moved around the country a bit. It wasn't even as if I had the girls at home as they had gone to boarding school several years ago.

'It was just me and his dogs rattling around in the house waiting for him to come home or to get some shore leave.

'Then when he finally came home and started this pub routine, I'll tell you what, you can be even lonelier when he is in the same room but on a different planet.'

The woman heaves a great sigh and gets up to make a cup of coffee. All these thoughts are churning around in her mind again and again. She can't say anything to anyone either. It would not be loyal. She can't even drink to forget. One of those in the family is enough. Besides, she has always had a cash register in her mind and after a couple of drinks it rings up 'enough'. Somebody has to be able to drive home anyway.

She gets her coffee and returns to her books. There is always plenty of marking to be done, let alone the books she is studying for her degree. Thank goodness for work, even though she is beginning to hate the stress of that too. When did she last feel relaxed? It is hard to remember. In fact, it is impossible. She is always on the alert, watching out for everyone, hoping to avoid trouble before it starts. It is not that he is belligerent. The only one he hurts is himself.

Sometimes he says, "At least, I have never raised my hand to you, even if I am drunk".

"Too right and you had better not," she mutters.

Still you can be hurt in more ways than physically. But you can't say that. It counts as nagging.

When they lie in bed and the snoring gets through to her, the tears that flow down her face and soak the pillow give some release to her feelings, and he doesn't even know. He wouldn't understand that big knot of loneliness that separates them even as they are together in the same bed.

Why had they reached this stage?

Chapter Two
Liz, Her Early Life

She had always been pretty independent. An only child, born just before the war. She had, perhaps, always been old for her years. She had been a companion to her mother while her father was at sea somewhere. He had also been in the Navy and, in her earliest years, it was wartime too. When she was five, they had gone to live in Scotland, in the back of beyond, three miles from the nearest school and 20 miles from the town.

A bright child, she had returned to her hometown with a broad Scots accent to confuse her grandmother and was a good year ahead of her contemporaries at her old school. She was happy to be at the top of her class and the leader in imaginative games in the playground. The other girls began to catch up and they all got on well as they came to the end of their junior school and took the 11+ exam.

Her father had been posted to Weymouth but Liz and her mum waited until after the exam before going down to join him for her last term as a junior. To her surprise, Liz found that she was only one of two in her class at a seaside school who had already learned to swim. At home, all the kids learned to swim in the rivers around the town. That was before the polio outbreak of course.

Liz had already passed her 11+ and started the next year in Weymouth Grammar School in the C stream. She learned a salutary lesson that teachers expected her at least to know the correct spelling of 'grammar'.

Her dad was like the matron of the Naval Hospital at Portland and when she went in with him on a Saturday morning, it was surprising how respectful his staff were towards him. He spoilt her rotten, of course, so it was interesting to see him in a different light. One of them told her that, "He is a stickler, but fair." It was an insight into both the discipline and management skills in the Navy, but she didn't appreciate that at the time.

Two significant things happened to her in Weymouth. She learned to roller-skate badly, and the local hedges bore witness to the fact that she had difficulty in stopping. She also went to the cinema and after watching a scary film about zombies she often woke up frightened by her dreams of them.

On return to her hometown when her Dad was posted abroad, Liz and her Mum became good friends. Liz found herself in the A-stream at her local school and found her spot at the top of almost every subject, except maths. She wasn't much good at games either and don't even mention domestic science. Schooldays were a very happy time, and she didn't mind being called a swot as there was no rancour in it. The boy who beat her at maths did tend to crow over it though.

When they were 14, the children of the town and surrounding villages were able to attend the youth club in the centre of the town. This was incredibly important in their young lives as, under the kindly eye of the youth leader, young people under the age of 21 met together to chat, listen to music and dance to records or the local group of boy musicians. It was a friendly, alcohol-free environment and the rules were kept. The grammar school kids met others who left school at 15 and went out to work. The ones from the west of the town met those from the bottom of town and those from the villages. It was the first mixing pot and an introduction to the wider world.

The world got even wider when the youth leader was invited to take part in a youth exchange with a town in Germany as part of a plan to break down the prejudices of the war which had ended just ten years earlier and people were still suffering on both sides. The first visit was by a party of German young people, who came to England just before the end of the summer school term so really only those hosting the young Germans were very much aware of it. The schoolchildren were in the thick of exams at that time. O-level exams were taken at the end of two years study and everyone else in the school had exams to keep them quiet!

The school leaving age was 15 but not for those taking exams. They had to stay to the end of the year when they were 16 and only a handful went on into the sixth form to do A-levels or for a year's secretarial course. Many of the boys from the grammar school left to take up apprenticeships and continue studying on day-release at the further education college ten miles away. The end of the fifth form year was the time when many friends went their different ways. They had been together since they had started school at five years old, boys and girls separate until they joined at the grammar school. It might be many years until they would meet up again.

Members of the youth club still had a chance to meet together for a few more years but this was really the true launching point into adult life. You were not really grown-up and a card-carrying adult, able to vote or to get married without parental consent until you reached 21 but for many, this was the time of independence and time to leave the parental home. For those continuing studies, you still needed parental support and approval.

The return visit to Germany took place in this crucial year, and Liz, who had started to learn German at school, was determined to go. She was the second youngest in the group, apart from the daughter of the youth leader, and for nearly all of them, it was the first time they had been abroad, especially, without their parents. The journey was endless, by coach to Dover, ferry to Ostend and then by a train that waited in the middle of the night in Cologne station until the other half of it joined from Paris. Then, they travelled northwards again. The train had wooden seats and an overhead luggage net and was not very comfortable. The final part of the journey was by a small local train. In all, they travelled for nearly thirty hours, and they were very pleased when they arrived and met the families who would host them for the next week or so. The English boys and girls were very pleased to find that the children in the host families spoke quite good English even if their parents didn't, and they were soon scattered throughout the town.

Liz was pleased that she got on well with both of the girls in the family she stayed with and found that her few words of German helped her to communicate with their baby brother and their parents.

It was in Germany that she fell in love for the very first time. Talk about sweet sixteen and never been kissed. There hadn't been time for that and, anyway, the boys at school were friends, or not, as the case might be, nothing romantic at all.

With her new German friend, it was mainly teasing each other, the occasional hand-holding, a kiss maybe and a promise to write.

The visit to Germany was another milestone in growing up: the long journey, staying with strangers, seeing new places, learning to communicate, drinking the odd beer, different kinds of dancing, Peter Stuyvesant cigarettes and much spluttering, different food and the realisation that a boy – a really nice and popular boy – could find her attractive.

She had long been resigned to gazing over the heads of boys she danced with at the youth club on the odd occasions they asked her to dance. Suddenly, at the magical age of 16, they began to grow taller, and she was beginning to have to look up to some of them. Life was changing.

The next year was a doddle, after the frantic O-level studies. They only did three A-levels and in small groups, so Liz was able to fit in further German lessons to go with her English, French and geography studies.

At Easter, she went on another trip abroad, this time to Paris, joining a mixed group of students from all over the country to stay in a French boarding school and learn proper pronunciation. She was mortified that she didn't even have to open her mouth before shopkeepers addressed her in English. There was obviously an image problem to overcome as well. She got on well with her fellow students on the trip but didn't pursue any friendships. One person to correspond with was enough and her German was improving slowly.

The second year, sixth, was a whole different ball game and the pace hotted up. There were also applications to universities and visits to some. Liz found that the standards expected were high and competition in the field she had chosen was fiercer than expected. Although French was her strongest subject, she couldn't get an offer to study it in the Universities she had chosen and only Newcastle offered her a place to study geography. That was a long way from home.

As a second string, she took the Civil Service exam and was offered a job in a central London office.

While awaiting A-level results, it was time for the next exchange visit to Germany. Liz had, of course, put her name forward again and this time there were several of her old school-friends coming too. Some had already started work, but the links through the youth club were still strong, and they met up at weekends for dances at home or away at other clubs.

It was a much more grown-up group this trip, having learned a lot from the pioneers. Aware of the travelling conditions, the girls wore trousers so they could prop their legs up the windows and perhaps get some sleep, and some of the boys even turfed out the cases and climbed into the luggage racks to sleep as if in hammocks. The Peter Stuyvesants were bought on the ferry and everyone had a puff or two.

Most people were staying with families, who had already taken part in the exchange and their children were two years better at English. Liz was still the only one of the group who spoke any German. She was staying with the girl, who had come the previous year to stay at her home and they knew each other very well.

There were the usual civic speeches that passed over everyone's head until the promise was made of tea, and there it came. Tea. No milk and no sugar. The English faces fell.

There was no sign of Liz's pen friend, Kurt. Since his father had died, he had to give up his law studies and go to work before starting studies to become a teacher. All was not lost, however, and Liz's hostess showed her how to sneak out of the ground-floor window and meet him late at night when he finished work. Liz lost quite a lot of sleep that week, but her German improved.

After another very successful exchange visit, it was the parting of the ways for many friends.

A-level results came together with County awards for university bursaries. Liz passed her A-levels but did not get a bursary. Her maths rival, however, had the last laugh. Those who were going to train to be teachers also had grants, but Liz decided to follow her second path and was off to London to the world of work.

Chapter Three
Work

From a small country town to the big city was quite a shock to the system. The Civil Service had a number of hostels for its new young employees and from being an only child, Liz found herself in a dorm with five other girls, who were working in various Government Departments. After spending years at school avoiding games, even by volunteering to run the library, Liz astonished herself by joining the Air Ministry hockey team when one of her room-mates recruited her and a girl working for the Foreign Office. To her great surprise, she enjoyed it.

Her own job was in a small Government Department where they tried to make use of her potential by putting her to work in the International Branch. She had never been so bored in her life. She wrote home to her parents pleading with them to pay to send her to university after all. Her father told her that it was too late. He had made the offer earlier and she had turned it down so now she would have to make a go of the Civil Service. So that was that.

Liz had to make the most of her time in London. She started evening classes, leading to further qualifications in French and German. She took advantage of all the cheap seats to all the theatres in London that were offered through the hostels. She soon knew just how hard was every upper circle seat in the city. Every day at work, she read *The Times* from cover to cover, read UN papers in both French and English, constructed programmes for visitors to see the working of the Department and would still be bored. She even read the *British Medical Journal* from cover to cover and wished she had not been intimidated by the biology master at school and had followed her other career choice of medicine instead of languages.

The reality of the world of work is that the speed of the convoy is that of the slowest ship and where that ship is your immediate boss you can spit out as many teeth as you like but things don't change. The secretary gave her a dictionary for Christmas, but she was only really stretched when her boss went on holiday, and she had her desk clear within a week. That didn't go down too well as there were months of files that had been waiting for attention. Soon after, Liz was moved to a different job.

This was more of a challenge as it was maths based. She soon realised that those she was supposed to supervise had it cracked, as they had been doing the job for years, and she was only needed for liaison and to be the front-man, or woman. Her opposite number in the distant office had a friendly voice and their conversations were the highlight of the week. Her staff thought she was good because she trusted them and the only hiccup was on election day when they were discussing who to vote for, and she had to admit that she was still too young to vote.

So what happened to her love life during this period? Not a lot, I'm afraid, as when she found that a boy was coming on too strongly, she backed off at great speed. She made one or two friends outside of work and fortunately had two good friends in the same building, who had joined at about the same time as she had. They had been the first new blood for about ten years, so they tended to keep together as the next ones at their level were in different offices, like the one who phoned Liz with the weekly figures.

Liz had moved to a new hostel near the British Museum and could walk to work straight down Holborn in the mornings but back through Soho at night, stopping for coffee or to pick up some delicatessen.

However, Liz had had enough of living in the city and realised she was a country girl at heart. She went home many weekends for a breath of fresh air and Mum's cooking. When the chance came to apply for a transfer to a new office in Hampshire, she jumped at it.

The new job as PA to the head of operations was just what she needed – a chance to have her finger on all the different aspects of all the work in that location. She thrived on it. She even met her telephone friend who had also transferred to Hampshire to head up one of the sections. There was also a social club which needed to be organised.

The only potential problem was that the new job was near Portsmouth, Gosport and thousands of sailors in training camps. Sailors! Her dad had been a sailor. Oops!

The job was going well, and there were lots of young people about, school leavers and naval wives. Liz even recruited her old school friend who was married to a sailor and living in the area. She had a small child and Liz went over to visit once a week, taking a half-a-dozen eggs so that she wouldn't be a strain on the household budget. Always that independent streak.

The first year flew by. In the summer, Liz and one of her new friends decided to go to Germany, travelling in local trains, hitch-hiking, staying in youth hostels. They travelled across the North Sea and then down to stay with her girlfriend's family in the German twin town before heading further south.

Correspondence with Kurt had tailed off the previous year, but both of them had been busy. Liz and her English friend found Kurt at home, and he invited them in for coffee and a chat. He said he had just got engaged to a fellow teacher. Liz offered her congratulations and hoped they would have a very happy life together. So that was that. End of her first romance. They had been good friends for six years but that was not enough to overcome living in different countries.

The following day, Liz and her travelling companion headed for Hamburg and the Rhine Valley. It was interesting to see Cologne by daylight after all those night-time visits when the train had its long wait. They had a few lifts but felt safer travelling by local bus and train and the steamers on the river. Staying in the youth hostels was fun and they enjoyed all the sightseeing. It was so different from Hampshire. Suddenly it was time to return home, as their time was up and they had to head for the Channel and home.

Liz threw herself into work and the social club. The office had a lot of female staff and the naval establishments ran a lot of dances to which were invited 'nice gals' like nurses and civil servants to even up the numbers. There were few weekends when there were no invitations.

On blank weekends, there were public dances in Southsea or you could even go to the theatre or cinema.

There were some new young boys who had recently joined the office, but they seemed terribly young and Liz was beginning to feel her age. Playing bar billiards with them was all very well but Liz was almost on the shelf with no regular boyfriend. Even the young friend who had come to Germany with her was talking about getting engaged. Liz would just have to shake herself off and go out seriously looking for 'The One'.

There had been one or two fumbles after dances, and once it had developed into more than a fumble, it was 'back off quickly'. She really hadn't found anyone as special as Kurt had been.

Had she always been too independent? Were her expectations too high?

Chapter Four
In the Beginning...

Then she went to another Naval dance, and there he was.

Across a crowded room – she spotted him.

There was a group of lads at the bar. Where else? They seemed to be having a good time listening to an account about something that was making them fall apart with laughter. The storyteller had dark blonde wavy hair and seemed to be popular with his mates.

Liz was definitely interested. He was far more handsome than the others and seemed to have a bright personality as well. It was frustrating in the extreme just to sit there, fingers crossed and hope that he would notice her too. She hadn't seen him before, though some of the others had been at several recent dances. At last, there was a movement at the bar. They must have had a sufficient number of drinks to build up some Dutch courage to think about dancing.

It was always the same at the beginning of the evening. For the first hour or so, the girls sat and waited hopefully until the first brave couple took to the floor and others got the courage to seek a partner to join them. Sometimes, the girls got fed up and danced together, hoping that a pair of males would come to break them up. That option wasn't open to Liz, as she had come alone that evening, so she just had to sit there, the original wallflower.

Someone was coming towards her. She had to hold still and pretend she hadn't noticed and was listening intently to the band. There was nothing worse than lighting up a smile only to find he had walked right past you. "Would you like to dance, Liz?"

It was one of the lads she had met before and he even remembered her name. That was an advantage in being one of the organisers of a social club. She stood up with a smile and he took her hand and led her to the dance floor. He was quite a good dancer and the circled round giving Liz the chance to look at the room. He was still at the bar.

"Who is your friend over there, Harry? Are you all at the same camp?" Simple question, expressing interest. It was all she could do at this point as after all she was dancing with someone else. Harry told her that they were nearly at the end of the same course and had been together for a year. No wonder they were as thick as thieves.

When the music ended, Harry took Liz back to her seat and re-joined his friends. Liz didn't actually hear her name mentioned but knew they were talking about her. She was glad that her hair was behaving itself this week, all piled on top of her head and secured with packets of hair-pins to keep it in place. She hoped her lipstick had not come off yet.

Another dance started and Liz heard somebody approaching from the direction of the bar. It was hard not to turn round. She held her breath.

"Would you like to dance?" An even brighter smile this time as she rose to her feet. He was not as tall as Harry but still taller than her and now she could see him up-close, definitely good looking. It was a fairly slow quickstep (most tunes were quickstepped to, whether they were meant to be a fox-trot or even a waltz) and they were able to introduce themselves. "I'm Will," he said, "and you are called Liz, according to my friend, Harry."

"Right! And you are all on the same course at Sultan, I gather."

Who needs any more introductions? That was practically a life history. They carried on dancing until the music stopped and he led her over to a table. "I'll get us a drink," he said and disappeared towards the bar before Liz could say, "Thanks, I'll have a…"

Will re-appeared with two pints of lager. "There was no need to mess about with small drinks as the bar is so busy, so I brought a pint for each of us," he said, pleased with himself. So Liz had her first ever pint of lager.

They sat there, nursing their big glasses and beginning to talk when the music was not too loud. He didn't even go back for another drink until, suddenly, it was five to midnight and the band began to play the last waltz.

"Come on! It's the last dance," said Liz, holding out her hand. She didn't want anyone else to claim her as traditionally the ones who danced the last waltz walked home together. Will got to his feet, even leaving an inch of beer, and they moved close together. Never mind the dance steps. This was always a slow stagger round together, arms around the waist and perhaps the odd kiss. You had to be careful who you danced this one with.

"Where do you live?" he asked when the music stopped.

"I live in Gosport, but I came in my car," she replied. It was about five miles to where she was living with her aunt's sister. Now, would Will just see her to the car park or risk her driving him back to the garage and then see her home?

How else would he know where she lived? Will folded himself into the passenger seat of the mini and they drove home. Yes, the goodnight kiss was worth waiting for and she slipped into the house, leaving him with the long trudge back to camp.

Next day came the realisation that although they had talked a lot, they had not actually agreed to meet again. Still, at least he knew where she lived even if they had not got round to surnames or phone numbers.

It was a long week and so was the next. At the end of the third week, there was a Friday night dance at the camp where the lads were serving, so Liz decided to go with some other friends from work. She really hoped it hadn't just been a one night thing and she would see him again. She didn't dare look too hard to see if he was there, for he might have been with someone else. Most of his friends seemed to be at the bar, but no Will.

There were lots of other young sailors after all. Most of the camp seemed to be there. Most but not all. The one she particularly wanted to see was missing. As one of quite a jolly group of girls, Liz was dancing most of the evening.

When Harry asked her to dance again, she couldn't resist asking about Will. Harry looked a bit embarrassed and muttered something about unfinished business, but added that he did hope to see her again. So she had to make do with that. They changed the subject and talked about the course and where

Harry hoped to go next. He was expecting to get a ship, and since they were nearly all in Plymouth, he would be leaving the area. Not much hope really.

She left before the last dance and drove slowly back to her garage. As she was closing the doors, she noticed the flicker of a match as somebody lit a cigarette. She was being watched.

"Who is it and what do you want?" she called.

"It's only me. I wanted to see you. Are you on your own?" It sounded like Will's voice as far as she could remember.

"What do you want?" she repeated, clutching her keys in her fist. It was the only defence she had, not even a handbag that evening.

He came out of the shadows a bit hesitantly. "Can we talk?"

"I suppose so. Why were you not at the dance with your friends?"

"I sent you a message," he said.

"Yes, I saw Harry, but he was a bit vague," she was still on her guard.

"I wasn't sure how things would go and I had stuff to clear up."

"That is still pretty vague. What sort of things?"

He came over and put his arm around her, still holding the cigarette in the other hand. They drifted over to a low wall to sit on and sat for a while in silence. He threw the cigarette away and immediately went for another. He offered her one and lit them both.

"It's like this," he began, "there was this woman I was seeing over the Hill. Lots of money and a big house and liked younger men… At the time I thought 'What the hell…' I'd had a rough few years and could do with a bit of fun, meals out, free drinks and the like. She even let me drive her car."

"I didn't know you could drive," said Liz.

"I can't really, at least not legally. I haven't got a car licence. I used to have a big motor bike."

He was quiet for a few minutes, thinking.

"Then I met you, and well, I wanted to get things straight. I've been over there this evening and told her it's all over. She didn't seem all that bothered. I suppose she can always get another young man. I doubt if I was the first and I'm sure I will not be her last. That's what we were all laughing over that evening when I met you. I was telling my friends about being a rich woman's darling!"

There was a long silence.

"Too much information. I suppose I've blown my chances with you now. I'm so sorry. I really think I like you…an awful lot."

She digested this. The attraction was mutual. She really liked Will. He might even be 'The One'.

"That's quite a story. What do you expect me to say?"

"I'm trying to be square with you. Won't you give me a chance?"

She leaned over and gave him a peck on the cheek.

"It's Saturday already. Shall we go to Southsea this afternoon and walk a bit? Aunt Lou is expecting me home about now after the dance finished about an hour ago. Are you going to walk me home? We can talk later when I drive you out in my car. You will have to pass your test before you get your hands on my wheels."

So they made their first date.

Chapter Five
First Date – Liz's Story

I really didn't expect much that night, as, by the time I'd slipped indoors, removed my shoes and crept upstairs to my bedroom, my mind was churning with far more questions than answers. You have no idea how pleased I was that he had turned up at the garage if not at the dance, however, the things he had told me were full of loose ends. For instance, why had a lad like that needed to seek out the attention of an older woman when he could probably have had his pick of younger girls. Like me, for instance. Why had the last few years been so rough for him?

What would happen at our next meeting?

I had never made any great effort to encourage the men who passed by my life. I had enjoyed the company of some I'd met in London but not for long. I suppose, I was too fussy. I was in my 25th year and apart from Kurt, I had not really had a serious boyfriend. It wasn't that I didn't like men, it was that, well, he had to be pretty special to attract my attention, and I had low tolerance of fools. Most of the young lads I met had little in the brains department, or if they had, they didn't use them as the aim on a night out was to get smashed and expect a girl to like them then. The older ones who had something about them were either married or spoken for and I wasn't in to fighting an 'other half'.

I suppose I was in the 'tween age' for my generation…not quite on the shelf, though many of my school friends were married. I was horribly independent, decidedly fussy but had not yet decided to fit the career-girl mould.

This Will, though, intrigued me. He was obviously a sociable man so why had he not been snapped up? What had led him to being the 'toy-boy' of the rich woman he had just finished with? He didn't seem the avaricious type, in fact quite the opposite. He seemed to really care what I thought about him. The most important thing, of course, was that he had made the effort to come and see me again. There is nothing so attractive as being liked by someone.

My thoughts whirled. I thought I'd never get to sleep.

When I woke up, it was nearly mid-day and I needed to have a bath and get ready to go out as he was coming at 2 pm (before Aunt Lou got home from work). I didn't need any complications at that stage.

I dressed in ski-pants and a sweater. I didn't think we would be going dancing that evening and for walking by the sea or going for a drink that would be the best outfit. I always kept a jacket or two in the car. My little red mini was part of my wardrobe.

I had a cheese sandwich and a glass of milk for brunch. I could last for hours on that.

"Gosh! Two o'clock already. What have I got in my handbag? Am I ready now? Better drop in a lipstick in case it doesn't stay on. Is that the doorbell? Right, I'm all set."

He was standing on the doorstep dressed in civvies…slacks and a tweed jacket…so that matched my outfit. If anything, he looked almost as anxious as I felt. We smiled at each other and I came out, checked the keys were in my bag and shut the door behind me. At the gate, he took my hand as we walked to the garage.

"Did you get back alright last night?"

"Yes, but it is quite a walk and my cat was waiting to see me."

"I didn't think you were allowed to keep animals when you are in barracks. You are in barracks aren't you?"

"I'm not really allowed, but she is a stray and comes and goes through my window. Lucky that I live on the ground."

An animal lover…that is a plus point. No doubtful answers today.

"She reminds me of the cat I used to have at home, a grey tabby. I call her Mogs. My mum died…"

"I'm sorry," I said and we walked on a while in silence.

"I suppose it is still alright to go to Southsea this afternoon, as the weather isn't bad?"

"Wherever you like. You're the driver! Though I must say, I have never been taken out for a drive by a girl before."

"You're OK, I've only written-off one car."

I opened the garage door and backed out my mini as he went to close the door and the padlock. It was quite nice to have somebody to do that for me. He climbed in and I waited until he had put on the belt before I set off. I must say he didn't look too happy as a passenger, but then I hated to be driven by most other drivers. Perhaps, I shouldn't have told him I'd had a crash. The mini is a small car in traffic, especially when you get between two buses, and I must admit that I had rarely seen a man in the passenger seat with a lady-driver. I expect Will was a bit embarrassed by that too.

After a mile or two, we were settling down and the traffic wasn't too bad at that time of day, so we could begin a conversation. We passed the hall where we had met.

"Do you know, that was the first time I had ever had a pint of lager," I murmured.

"Why, what do you usually drink?"

"Oh, Cinzano or Martini or something and cider if I want a long drink. I'm a West Country girl".

"I'm sorry, I didn't think to ask. I just wanted to get us a drink and get back to you before someone else took you off."

How sweet. He was certainly not aware of my wallflower tendencies. Dance partners were not usually that eager, probably because in heels I was taller than a lot of the lads, and I had quite cultivated that distant look. Still, he had approached me from behind.

"I quite enjoyed the lager. It's thirst quenching. I'd drink it again." So started a trend.

I sneaked a sideways glance then back to the traffic again. The road was never less than busy and in peak times it was a nightmare, but at this time on a Saturday, it was fairly clear and soon we were parking down by the beach. I reached into the back for my jacket as it was quite breezy.

It must be because my dad is a sailor that I absolutely love being by the sea. Walking beside it or just sitting and watching the waves lapping is just great. When you have a handsome man beside you, it is even better than usual.

Soon, we were chatting away. Will's home was in the North, but he had no parents there as his father had been killed in the war and his mum died the year before we met. He had two brothers, one older who had just come out of the Navy and one younger who was also a sailor and out in the Caribbean somewhere. I had my parents back home but no brothers or sisters.

Then, he dropped the bombshell.

"I'm still married, though legally separated." He turned towards me looking really anxious. "I had to be up-front with you. I didn't want you to hear about that from anyone else."

Silence. I needed to digest this bit of news. He dropped his arm from my shoulders. "I suppose I had better go."

I should have expected something like this as he was older than me and, as I said, rare to find a good looking man who was not already spoken for.

"Will, you have been really straight with me. I don't want to see you go. Let us go on and walk some more while I think things over."

It was probably not the first time I'd been out with a married man, in fact I know it was not, but this felt different. By the time we had walked all along the promenade and back to the car, I was sure I didn't want it to end there and neither did he. The wind was getting up and we decided to go to a pub for a drink and a meal. I'd provided the transport, so I had no qualms about being treated to steak and chips.

I made my half of lager last a long time and the last thing that Will wanted was to drink too much at this very delicate stage in our friendship.

We drove back the pretty way, up over Portsdown Hill and I pulled in at the top of the hill so that we could see the city lights way below. It was a well-known place for courting couples, though a mini is a bit restrictive. We managed, however, and by the time I switched on the ignition again, I had been well and truly kissed. He was pretty good at that. Most of the pins had come out of my hair and I had not a trace of lipstick, but Hey! It was dark outside and soon coming up for Halloween.

We put the car away and he walked me back to the house. Our bodies fitted together quite well for that good-night kiss, but the lights were still on and I hadn't seen Aunt Lou for several days. She was obviously waiting up for me.

"See you tomorrow, about ten. Goodnight, Will."

"Night, my love."

Had I heard a'right?

"Hello, Aunt Lou. You still up? I've been out with that PO I met at the club a couple of weeks ago. We are going out for the day tomorrow, so I shall have to be up early for a Sunday. It's alright, we are going in my car."

Chapter Six
Courting

The weather remained good on Sunday, so they went to the New Forest. Liz hadn't done so much walking in a long while. Well you don't if you are on your own. Will enjoyed being out in the countryside, and it was good to get out of town together.

At work, Liz had been arranging a Tramps' Ball for Halloween, and the social club had sent out reciprocal invitations to all the Naval camps to thank them for their invitations. Arranging that had been interesting, as well as her normal duties, of course.

Will was coming now, with several of his mates, and she was looking forward to introducing him to all her friends at work. He had borrowed some hobnail boots from a friend to give the authentic tramp look. Most were just wearing jeans and old sweaters to look scruffy. Once everything was underway, Liz went over to talk to them.

"I'd ask you to dance, Liz, but my feet are killing me in these boots."

"That's no excuse," she laughed. "Here, borrow my shoes, I can go just in my socks or barefoot." She kicked them off. She didn't mind dancing in her socks as it would give her a chance to show him off to all her Office friends. They had already noticed that she looked happy and had heard of the new boyfriend.

Will discovered that they had something else in common. The same size feet. He was quite comfortable in Liz's shoes and his pained expression was changed for a smile. The girls, who had heard quite a lot about him, gave the vote of approval.

Sometimes they went out with friends, sometimes to the cinema, for a walk or for a drive. Time flew by and at

Christmas, Will went to stay with his brother and Liz went home. They were both pleased when the holidays were over.

Will had started another course at Sultan so sea time was put off. He was really working hard now as he had new incentives to do well. Neither of them had a lot of money to spare, as Liz had her car to run and Will was taking driving lessons. Sometimes, they went out with her friends or they went alone to the cinema or just for a walk along a beach. Once Will had passed his test, he was allowed to drive Liz's car sometimes, but she preferred not to be a passenger in the mini. It was hers.

As the days grew longer, they were able to go further afield and Liz took him up to meet her parents. The two sailors looked almost like father and son as they both had a slight nautical roll and a touch of embonpoint. Mother's cooking or mess dinners.

Will took Liz down to Lulworth to visit his father's grave.

Despite the obstacles, they were growing closer and didn't like time apart.

Liz got a bit concerned. Things had never been this serious before. They had passed the 'boyfriend girlfriend' stage. In fact, one cool evening they had been sitting in front of the fire while Aunt Lou was at work, and they were kissing and cuddling until things got a bit heated when suddenly Will sat up. He took a French letter out of his pocket and threw it on the fire and said that he wasn't going to carry them any more as the temptation was too great and he didn't want their relationship to go that way and be spoiled. Liz knew that condoms were standard issue to all sailors going ashore, so she knew that Will was really serious.

Perhaps, they ought to stop now and wait until Will was free, but he had to wait several years to divorce his wife who had been unfaithful while he was at sea. Did she want to be on her own again?

Liz had booked a holiday abroad before they had really got too close. As the time drew near, Will got more and more miserable as he had no holiday plans. Perhaps she should take that opportunity to break things off? She had a cheap ferry crossing to Denmark again and intended to go up to Sweden and Norway this time. When she said this to Will, he was most upset and burst into tears. He was not the emotional type so she had really hurt him.

He really didn't want to lose her. The alternative was that he too should get a ferry crossing and then they could go together. Well, nearly. There was Liz in the cheapest cabin, sharing with three other females and there he was, travelling first class as that was the only accommodation left. They were both dressed for youth hostelling in jeans, sweaters and rucksacks.

The North Sea was not kindly and almost everyone was terribly sick. There was one notable exception in the first class dining room who worked his way through the entire breakfast menu as the stewards watched, amazed. One other passenger managed a cup of coffee. He was a sailor too.

It was on this trip that they realised that they were both in love and that the relationship was for keeps.

***

Liz takes up the story:

Everywhere we looked there seemed to be his and hers wedding rings in the jewellers shops, but since he was still married, all I got was a pendant necklace. It was just what I wanted to remember this holiday, really, and the stone was an alexandrite, which matched the one in my mum's favourite ring.

We stayed in youth hostels, tried to have one cooked meal a day and the rest of the time there was bread and cheese and bottles of fizzy. What more could you want? The trains were to carry us to all the Scandinavian capital cities, and we had booked ahead for all the youth hostels. Our first stop was Copenhagen and I remember visiting the Tivoli gardens, riding on trams and meeting lots of young people who came over from Sweden for the weekend to visit the Carlsberg brewery. Then we moved on to Sweden and headed for Stockholm.

By the time we arrived, the youth hostel was full and we were directed to a hotel which was running a special deal for displaced hostellers. We would never have dreamed of entering its doors if it hadn't been for that. It looked very expensive.

We were given the plushest hotel room I had ever seen, with a vast double bed and an en-suite bathroom. There we were, after a week travelling, scruffy, dirty and still armed with a loaf of black bread and smelly cheese. I couldn't believe our good luck. A deep scented bath was just what I needed to feel human again and then take it from there. While I unpacked our supper (there was no way we could have afforded to go into the dining room), Will ran me a bath. I didn't like to tell him it was hot enough to cook me even after we had eaten.

After my bath, I wrapped myself in big fluffy white towels and while Will had his bath, I crawled into bed. Pure luxury! There was no comparison with the narrow and hard bunk beds in the youth hostels. My eyes were closed and I didn't see Will come out of the bathroom and come over to the bed. He climbed in and put his arms around me and I curled into his body. This would be the first time that I had spent the night in the same bed as a very loving man. I turned towards him with a sigh and we sought each other's lips. Soon, I was being kissed most thoroughly, and my nightie was an encumbrance.

"Hang on a minute," I murmured as I struggled to take it off. I had help.

I was soon being kissed in places where I had never been kissed before, and my body liked it. I was rising to meet his lips and trying to kiss the bits of him that were available. There was a tingling deep inside of me and my blood was singing. What would come next? I wanted more.

Kissing in the mini had scarcely prepared me for this.

"Will, please make love to me, properly."

He raised his head and looked into my eyes. "Do you really mean it, Liz? I haven't got anything with me."

"Just love me, Will. This is a very special night. I want you."

That was an understatement. He had made my whole body reach out for him. He couldn't stop now as he had always done before. Here and now had to be the first time for us.

"I love you, Liz, and I have wanted you so much."

In the morning, as we stirred from an exhausted sleep, still wrapped in each other's arms. I couldn't resist the question, "Was it alright?"

"Like an old married couple," he replied with a grin.

I took that as a compliment, as I really had no idea of what making love could be like. It bore no resemblance to the quick fumbles I had met before. You really had to give yourself to the other, putting their pleasure before yours and in so doing, your joy was increased when it was reciprocated. It was all a question of trust

We couldn't spend time thinking about the previous night, time was passing. We hurried to get our things together and get away before we got charged for another day. Sweet though it had been, we had a train to catch.

Our journey through Sweden passed through forests and by lakes with flocks of ducks. The railway station buffets did a very good line in Wiener schnitzel. This was lucky as we found that we had left behind our emergency supply of bread and cheese at the hotel. I wonder what the maid thought.

Our next stop was in the middle of nowhere with a hike of about three miles to the youth hostel. We had to buy new emergency supplies. Ham and bread this time. It was only as we made our sandwiches at the hostel that we read the small print. 'Cook for ten minutes'.

We stayed in a room with four bunks. Although we had it to ourselves, it was not quite the same as being in the hotel.

All the other hostels had vacancies in single sex dorms, but the sightseeing was also an important part of the holiday. Soon it was time to return back to normality via the North Sea, me in the anchor locker, or very nearly, and Will in the first class again. Fortunately, this time the sea was calm.

There would never be another holiday quite like that.

My friends remarked on my sparkling eyes, my new necklace and commented that I seemed to have had a very good holiday.

I was, however, very relieved when my period came the following week.

Our relationship had changed as a result of the holiday. We were very sure of ourselves and our love for each other. It was very difficult to get back to the light but caring attitude that we had before even though we spent a lot more time with our friends.

Inevitably, however, our love overcame our good intentions and this time it was the wrong time of the month.

I was to be bridesmaid and Will best man at my friend's wedding. It was difficult to get my dress to fit. I had missed a month and despite hot baths and even gin (ugh!) I realised that one day, I should have to admit to impending motherhood. I shuddered to think what my parents would say. This career-girl, this know-all, this independent woman who had just become the youngest in the office to get promoted to the next grade, this silly girl had just landed herself in trouble and couldn't even get married.

I looked at the options and decided that we would have this baby. He or she would be much loved, and we would get married when we could.

We loved each other. Everything would turn out well. Eventually.

Chapter Seven
Now What? Liz Continues:

Our friends' wedding passed off successfully and suddenly Christmas was upon us. What should we do? Tell my parents and ruin their Christmas or ignore the situation and just make it a very short visit? Needless to say, I opted for the latter and explained that we were going up to Will's family for New Year, because, being northerners, that was the time when there were most celebrations.

It was time to go and meet his family, for we were now committed to each other come what may. I was delighted to belong to a larger family, with two brothers, a sister-in-law and their new baby girl. Soon, we would have one too. Could it be that my maternal instincts were stirring within this career girl? It had better be. We were both earning good money now, after promotions, so it was possible to go and look for a house. There would only be one earner soon as I would lose my job (you did in those days) and we would only have modest means. Our baby might have as yet unmarried parents but, she would certainly have a home and a home filled with love.

First, I had to brave my parents. Dad went ballistic when he heard that his daughter was not only pregnant but the father was still married. Mum was devastated, 'What will the neighbours say?' Will was of course banned from the house, so I went too. I hoped they would come round in time.

In the event, they bought a house before we could. My mother could not face the rumours and the embarrassment of having an unmarried mother for a daughter, so they moved out from the town where all their relations and friends lived and into a nearby village. For the first time in their lives, they bought their own house. It had formerly been the house where Mum's grandparents lived and they were able to buy it from her youngest aunt. When it was done up, it had a lot more room than the former one, that too was lucky as it turned out for 'Granny's House' played such an important part in our daughters' lives.

Our home came soon after. Will had been posted to Plymouth and was doing the weekend commute. The house came on the market on a Friday, and it was ours on the Saturday. There was no time to think things over. We viewed it in the dark, and there were one or two things we found later that needed doing, but apart from that it was just what we needed. It was a bungalow on the edge of the Naval area, not far from my office and in an area with a village atmosphere. Our budget was limited and prices were beginning to go up, so we had already arranged a mortgage.

Finally, we exchanged contracts and it was ours. When we went to see it again, we could see that there was quite a garden that would soon be productive, a carport to dry washing , carpets that smelled of dogs' and cats' pee and a whole lot of defective power-points. Whatever had we bought?

But it was ours and we could soon be together – at least at weekends.

We started on the kitchen and I had my first introduction to a wallpaper scraper. There were two rooms that had to be ready before we could move in the kitchen and the lounge. The kitchen had at least five years grime in it (That was the age of the bungalow). As it led into the garden, I could foresee that there was where I would spend most of my time.

I spent a fortune on cleaning fluids and brushes. Nearly all the carpets had to be burnt, because of the incontinent animals of the previous owner but we couldn't afford to replace the hall one so that really needed cleaning. It was a dark colour and ever after, kept a strong aroma of Dettol. That was, at least, an improvement on what it had been before!

The kitchen was soon resplendent with a bright washable wallpaper with bunches of fruit as the pattern, a rush-mat design vinyl floor-covering and a small fridge waiting for the arrival of the baby. Will had even sold his precious stamp collection to buy that. The paintwork was bright orange and turquoise; the fashionable colours that year. We replaced the cooker and bought a twin-tub washing machine while I still had some income from work. Will moved in his sleeping bag, and we sat on the floor, but we had our first room ready.

The lounge also had to be papered. It somehow made the rooms look more established and warmer. A lot of houses just had painted walls but ours had a bright green vine patterned paper which was very distinctive. In later years, whenever I saw a house with the same paper, I was reminded of those early days and all the hope and effort we put into our first home. It was a good thing that I married a practical man. I wouldn't have known where to start.

I was still at work, wearing increasingly baggy jumpers and trying to pretend that all was well. Then there was a major snowstorm and the only house I could get home to was up the road, our new bungalow. I managed to get the mini into the drive, but the increasing depth of snow meant I was going no further.

We had begun to scrape off the old wallpaper and so had water, electricity and a kettle. The camp bed that Will had been using at weekends was not very comfortable, but any port in a storm. And what a storm! I couldn't get the car out but struggled in to work the next day, and I looked so ghastly that I had to confess to my pregnancy and imminent, so we still hoped, marriage. After that, life was easier and I had time off to go the antenatal classes and booked my maternity leave after which my job would end.

My colleagues offered congratulations and advice. The best advice, which I took, was that when buying a carpet the pattern should be multi-coloured to hide the spills and accidents of babyhood, especially blackcurrant juice and baby-sick. How I blessed that one!

I ordered the carpet from a place where I could get a discount and the other basic furniture from catalogues. I was not too proud to accept hand-me-downs, especially curtains and the ones Mum gave me must have come from her grandma's time. The cats' pee carpet had long been evicted and the decoration was going on apace. Will came home at weekends and returned to duty absolutely exhausted. He was a perfectionist and even when I was allowed to help with some of the basic painting he supervised every stroke of the brush. This house was going to be perfect.

I had handed in my notice 'in expectation of my forthcoming marriage'. I hoped it would be possible to reclaim my pension contributions if it happened within six months but the wheels of the divorce courts were turning very slowly. There seemed to be so much to get to set up home properly. I ordered what I could from a store where I could get a discount and essentials by mail order.

I acquired my grandmother's old sewing machine to make curtains and things. I was never very good at sewing but someone had to do it, and we certainly couldn't afford to buy ready-mades.

Mum and Dad came round a bit and donated curtains and linen as they realised that we were determined to succeed. Dad still wouldn't speak to Will though. He still wouldn't trust him to stand by me until we were actually married – not even with a house as evidence of good intentions.

I suppose it was my money that paid the deposit, but once I left work all the expenses would fall on Will's shoulders. Sailors knew what sailors could be like I suppose.

Despite everything, we were happy to see our home coming together and as soon as I left work for maternity leave, I was able to leave Aunt Lou's house and move into our own. I'd stayed on for appearances sake until then but suspected that she was the source of the rumours that had caused Mum to move out of town. Every penny would count now as young mums were not expected to work. Fortunately, we had achieved everything we had set out to by that stage.

It was good to get out of my baggy jumpers and into a real summer maternity dress, courtesy of my sewing skills, and to be able to have a rest in the afternoon and really concentrate on the coming baby. There was still some work to do on the house but the furniture arrived, well most of it. The bed base arrived but no mattress. There had been a mix up and there was a three month delay. That was cutting it more than a bit fine! What a good thing we had ordered a suite with a sofa bed.

Since the bed had not arrived, we had no excuses for not decorating the main bedroom and putting in some built-in wardrobes. I was really pleased that we had bought a DIY handbook for Will. I wasn't so sure about the cookery book for me though. The nursery was also finished, even if I did have to sit on a chair to finish some of the painting. I was really getting tired and awkward in these last few weeks. It was even getting difficult to get behind the wheel of the mini to go to my antenatal classes.

The kitchen was still the last room to be completely finished and Will asked his younger brother for help putting up ceiling tiles. They looked really good by the time it was finished late that night. The next morning, they were all on the floor so they had to start again with more glue.

It was exciting getting the house together and picking the things for the nursery. All in yellow, though I had long been convinced she would be a girl. When the smell of June strawberries was all around, the baby was due.

Mum came down to stay with me as Will was still in Plymouth, and I didn't want to be on my own for the last week. Thank goodness the mattress finally arrived and she could have the bedroom while I still had the sofa-bed in the lounge. Dad brought her down then disappeared off home as I still was not entirely forgiven. I hoped that after the baby arrived, he could be friends with Will as they were so alike in many ways.

It was lovely, warm weather and we were out in the garden when I felt the first pains. I'd been advised that it might take some time so I took Mum for a stroll to the library. We came back at a much faster pace as, by then, I could no longer ignore what was happening, and Mum had noticed too.

I rang the maternity home where I had been booked in. "Sorry, closed to new admissions." Panic was rising for Mum let alone for me. We were referred to another hospital which was nearer, so that was good and we rang for a taxi.

It was pretty busy there too and I was put into a bathroom to await my turn and Mum was sent home. It might not have been the most comfortable place, lying on the cover over the bath but the baby didn't know that and continued to make her way into the world more rapidly than expected. I could hear a lady nearby screaming at the top of her voice and, to me, that seemed like a really good idea. When the midwife eventually came, I was moved into the delivery room. Having a baby was not an elegant procedure when your legs get put in stirrups and there is no way you can see what is going on down there. At last, she was born, my little girl. Not a very big baby, but I felt she must have come out sideways as I waited to be seen to and stitched up. Ann was ours. I couldn't wait to tell Will but they were at sea so I had to be patient for a few days.

The big surprise was when Dad came down with a bunch of roses. At last, the lure of a grand-daughter had brought him back to me and he stayed with Mum until Will was due home. He was still not forgiven.

Sadly, I proved to be a 'poor cow' as the doctor phrased it so accurately and Ann became a 'Carnation baby' as the tinned milk was readily available. At least, anyone could give her a feed.

I was glad of the two-week hospital stay, that was then the norm, as babies were a complete mystery to me having been a child with no siblings and only two cousins. I also didn't feel too good with a fluctuating temperature, but I supposed that was only to be expected. At least, I could share the feeding of Ann with Will when he came home on leave when I left the hospital.

Dad collected Mum then, and Will, Ann and I had a fortnight together, just the three of us. And the raspberries. They ripened just at that time and were Will's favourite jam. I'd never made jam before, but I learned. I could have done without it at that time, but couldn't waste our first harvest from the garden.

Will went back to the ship and I should have been fighting fit by then with such a contented baby, but I certainly was not. I should have been on top of the world for the pain of childbirth is soon forgotten, but I had developed this nagging pain that, sometimes, had me doubled up. There was nobody to ask and I supposed that it was just one of those things about getting back to normal and I should just get on with things like a good naval wife does when her man is away. I'd had it on and off ever since Ann was born and even going out with her in the pram didn't take my mind off it. It is a wonderful way to make friends, pushing a pram.

I just didn't feel well. I should have been strong and healthy as I was before the birth, but I felt so weepy that even looking forward to Will being back for the weekend didn't help. On the Sunday, he packed the car full of baby things, a weeping woman and a sleeping child and delivered us to Granny's

House. Dad wouldn't even let him over the doorstep, so I had to take him to the train station to get back home before catching his lift back to Plymouth. I felt awful for letting him go like that, but I just couldn't manage on my own. I hoped that a couple of nights sleep would make me feel better, so I could go back on my own.

Mum was in her element fussing over her grand-daughter. Dad was delighted with the baby so that was a relief, but I wished he had not been so unkind to Will. I just hoped the pain would go soon.

I didn't get home again for eight months.

At first, it was quite good just to have the baby to look after while Mum did everything else.

My pain didn't go away, however, despite daily walks out in the countryside with the pram. Dad thought it was a psychological thing because my life was in such a mess, so he encouraged me not to worry and just enjoy being out in the fresh air leaving all the responsibility to him and to Mum. It was like being a child again, back under the parental roof.

For once, his nursing instincts were wrong, and I suddenly developed a really high temperature and couldn't stop shivering, so they had to call a doctor, and I was whisked off to hospital with pleurisy and a kidney infection, developed when Ann was born.

For a whole week, Dad was at my bedside in hospital while Mum got on with the caring for the baby, as well as everything else. I don't know what else he thought of while he was there, but he wasn't going to let his girl out of his paternal care until she was safely married.

When I came out of the hospital, I was able to ring home and Will paid a flying visit to put his mind at rest, but only saw me and avoided Dad. He took the car back as I had no use for it.

That was it, Dad had decided and there could be no arguments. I wasn't fit to argue for months, as the pleurisy had a long recovery time and, anyway, Will was at sea so I was dependant on him. He was sorry that he hadn't taken my pain seriously until it was too late, but I really wished he would let Will back into our lives, as I missed him so much now I was feeling better.

When the walking and fresh air had restored my health, it was approaching Christmas, and I was still ensconced in the parental nest, although I tried to do my bit to help Mum. She had been reluctant even to hand the care of Ann back to me, so there was not a lot I could do indoors and after my walks, I was bored. Dad took me out to help him on his first aid courses, but really, village life was a bit limiting. I was not encouraged to go back into town, in case I met someone and my 'shame' was revealed. The 'swinging sixties' had not hit our neck of the woods.

Dad was right in one way. The six month deadline had passed since I left my job, and I had no income of my own. He was taking care of his little girl.

On Christmas Eve, Will came up for the day, in my mini which he was now using for the Plymouth run, with paying passengers. He peered at our daughter and gave her a kiss then took me out for lunch before we encountered Dad. I wept bitterly that night, but my aunt who was staying for Christmas told me that at least I knew it would all be over one day, unlike her position. Her husband was never coming back as he had died a few years earlier.

It is only now that I can appreciate the depth of her grief.

In January, I received a phone call. "Liz, will you marry me in about six weeks' time?" Would I?!

His divorce had finally come through and would be final in six weeks. We were not only counting the days, the hours as well.

Ann didn't come to our wedding but stayed with her grandmother. My cousin and his fiancée took me down to the register office where Will met us, and they were witnesses as we were finally married. Then, we all celebrated with a meal in our own home. Lots more work had been done and the house was sparkling clean. The garden had been cultivated to within an inch of its life and was positively standing to attention. My cousin was most impressed. We went back and stayed for our honeymoon night in a hotel near my parents, and the following day Will was given the prodigal son treatment. That was good but we could scarcely wait to take our daughter home and resume life together, all three in our own home. Together at last.

It had been a long time but we were sure of each other, and after such a dodgy start to our marriage, we thought we had suffered all the ill-luck that was going, and we would only be stronger for it.

Chapter Eight
Early Years

Now that she was a properly married Naval wife, Liz was entitled to a regular housekeeping allowance or allotment out of Will's pay. She had four pounds a week to do everything except pay the mortgage which was deducted out of the bank account. The time had passed when she might have claimed repayment of her pension contributions, as there was too long a gap between leaving work and their marriage. They learned to live very frugally, but that was nothing new as they had both been wartime children.

Before their marriage and for many years after, she could think of no complaint about her husband. Other naval wives criticised theirs openly when they met for coffee mornings, but Liz could not join in such conversations. He was just a perfect husband, lover and father. He didn't even drink anymore as they couldn't afford it. As they cuddled up to each other in their warm home, with baby Ann asleep in her cot, they finally had a chance to talk to each other about their lives before they had met.

She had been a spoilt only child, but companion to her mother when her Dad was away. She had been academic and ambitious and expected to 'go places'.

Will, on the other hand, had been the middle of three brothers, practical by nature, and had taken on the role of scavenger and provider for the family as soon as he was able. After his father had been killed in the war, they had had to leave army accommodation and move back to his mother's parents. His grandfather was the one who taught him how to garden, the hard way, on his smallholding in Yorkshire. They had moved into the local town, and Will's mother, who had been a nurse, did home knitting while his baby brother was too small to be left.

One of the early presents he bought Liz, as a surprise, was a knitting machine since she had no skills in that department. She didn't have much skill with the machine either, but it kept the family in jumpers until they got too fussy.

Childhood for boys was very different from girls. In the summer, they seemed to range all over the hills from morning to dusk on only a jam sandwich and a bottle of water to keep them going. They were expert foragers and knew all the berries and fruits of the hedgerows and in season would bring home field mushrooms for tea.

As soon as he was old enough, Will got jobs as a butcher's and a greengrocer's delivery boy, so that the spoils at the end of the day could go home to help the family. He also dragged home the sacks of potatoes, he was allowed to keep, after the autumn potato-picking holiday. He loved his food, and Liz had to learn to cook properly, although she could never compete with the memories of trays of sausage rolls that his mother used to make.

At school, Will was interested in maths and practical subjects, so he went to the technical stream of the school. This led him to follow his elder brother into the Navy as soon as he was old enough. When his mother remarried, his brother's home became his new base.

In the Navy, he became a stoker and that was in the days of coal-fuelled ships, though they soon changed to diesel engines. He developed an enviable physique with hard work and playing water polo for the Navy. He really enjoyed time in Malta interrupted by the Suez war when he was sent to help to clear the Canal. Liz was still at school at the time.

His potential was recognised, and he was sent to upgrade his skills to be a mechanician and to remedy any gaps in his education by taking O-levels. He was proud of those.

Somewhere along the line, he had married a girl from his hometown, and he would never know how jealous Liz was of her name tattooed on his arm. "Young and very drunk sailors had tattoos done and that also accounted for the ring of roses across my chest," he said. While he was at sea she had been unfaithful to him, and it was with great bitterness that he had obtained a separation order. It was all a matter of trust. Serving sailors could be away from their families for months at a time, more than any other members of the armed forces, except in wartime, and naval wives had to be very special women, as Liz came to find out.

His younger brother was also divorced by the age of 21 for the same reason.

By the time that Will had completed his mechs' course, he was due for some sea time, and it was lucky that the ship had undergone a refit and trials before they had to go far away. Will had become ambitious with his new family and wanted to exceed the rank of his father-in-law. Sea time would give him studying time as well for his years were against him, and he had several hurdles to overcome before he was too old to be considered.

Liz had made some friends locally, including some near neighbours with children the same age, on the visits to the clinic and just walking in the village. A pram is a great ice-breaker, nearly as good as a puppy! Ann was becoming an attractive child with fair ringlets and brown eyes, interested in everything. Every week Liz met up with other young mums, as they took their babies to be weighed at the clinic. They were contented in their simple lifestyle, comfortable as a family even if only all together at weekends. Will was using the car for commuting to Plymouth and also to earn a little extra by taking fellow sailors on the same trip. Liz and Ann were together during the week staying around the village or visiting other naval wives whose husbands were also based in Plymouth. They sometimes had a real good moan about their husbands, but Liz could not join in. Will was just perfect. She was so lucky. He was the ideal husband, lover and father. She had no complaints. At weekends, he came home with the car and went for a major shop at the supermarket. He knew it so well he made his list according to the order of shelves he would pass and when all was done, they were free to enjoy time together.

As for Will, content with his new wife, he just doted on Ann and it was hard to drag himself away after a weekend, let alone for longer.

Then the ship set sail for the Far East and Liz and Ann were left on their own. They went round to the neighbours to visit and let the children play together while the mothers had a chat. At least, with the sole use of the mini, Liz could go and visit friends further away, go down to the sea or even go up to her parents for longer visits. They were, of course, very welcome as the rift was completely healed and her Dad couldn't get over baby Ann as, of course, he had been away in the war when Liz was that age and he had missed her babyhood entirely.

Parcels arrived from Singapore full of dainty dresses for Ann, as Will seemed to spend his spare time at the night market looking for treasures for his daughter.

Liz got no sympathy from her mother when she complained that he would be gone for a whole six months. "In my day, they went off for years at a time and with no airmail service for letters. We didn't know if they were alive or dead. You have no idea what it was like."

Of course she was right. Liz had her letters and her daughter to feel close to him, and she knew he would be back in six months to start the next course. Mum had been left with nothing in her early years, as they had been married for ten years before Liz was born.

There was more companionship and support for young naval wives in quarters, but that was for younger girls. Liz was proud that they had their own home and of the work they had put into it.

Occasionally, she met up with the wives of the men who had been on the same mechs' course as Will. Most of the husbands were putting in sea time now, waiting for the next step up. The wives took it in turn to be hostess and it gave the chance to give the best coffee cups an airing as usually she used a mug. It was hard to listen to all the moans about their menfolk and Liz just couldn't join in. Perhaps, it was that he was determined to make this marriage work after the first was a failure, but more likely he was just a good man. It was good to speak with the other Naval wives as the 'civvy' ones had no concept of the isolation they sometimes felt.

The time began to pass more swiftly.

At the coffee mornings, Liz realised how lucky she was with Will as she listened to the others complain about their husbands' inability to do this or tendency to do that. Some of them couldn't wait until their time was up and they could rejoin civvy life without all the interruptions when their husbands were posted somewhere else. For Liz, she couldn't imagine Will in any other career. He seemed to be in his element making things work and getting on with his team. It wasn't enough though. She encouraged his ambition.

When he returned, he came off the ship to the training school where he had been when they met. He had been promoted to C.P.O and this gave him entrance to the chiefs' mess at the engineering school where he had another course to do. The best naval chefs hold the rank of Chief and for someone who loved his food this was the place to be. Fortunately, a lovely couple lived next door and when there was a special dinner or dance on, they were more than happy to baby-sit. Liz and Will finally began to enjoy some social life and the buffets were a work of art. It felt good to get dressed up and go out, and Liz used the sewing machine she had acquired from her grandmother, to make curtains, to make some party clothes too. No way was she a skilled seamstress, but needs must. The dresses usually lasted a couple of wearings before they started to fall apart. Material could be bought in the market. Real shops were still a no go area.

It was a good summer for walks on the beaches and in the country and just to be together. They made the most of it. Liz was blooming. They had decided that Ann was most definitely not to be an only child and by her second birthday Liz was pregnant.

Will had to leave again at the end of the summer to get experience on a different type of ship, and he was off to the Far East again.

Liz and Ann were left on their own, but by now Ann was a little character in her own right, and Liz had little time to spare to keep the garden in order, and it showed.

Airmail letters and photos to show Ann's progress as a little girl were soon winging their way. Liz was convinced that the next baby would be a boy, and she started to knit baby things in blue. At least, a girl could wear light blue even if pink would be impossible for a boy, and the nursery was already yellow and green.

Will's younger brother came to visit and was thrilled with his golden haired niece with the family curls and took some stunning Polaroid photos to send to her Dad. Ann was a bit bemused by this uncle who looked like Daddy and sounded a bit like Daddy but was called Uncle. She enjoyed his company, so it was not just Liz who was missing Will.

Liz told herself that she should never have married a sailor for companionship for they were never there when they were really wanted. Will would be away for the birth of her next baby and already she was so big that she could scarcely fit into the mini. "I'm glad they have assured me it isn't twins," she said. She changed her mind and decided it would be another girl because she felt so fit this pregnancy and it would be good to have a companion for Ann.

As Christmas approached, Liz decided to pack up her house and move up to Granny's House, willingly this time. She didn't want to be caught by the bad weather and already could scarcely get behind the wheel. She would need help when the baby arrived and Mum and Dad were more than willing to have them.

Despite Will's absence, Christmas was altogether more cheerful this time with Ann running around and enjoying being spoilt at Granny's House. But Liz was determined to return home as soon as she could. The baby was in no hurry, however.

Liz was conscious of the extra work it put on her mother, even though she protested that it was no bother, and she tried to do what she could to help. Usually this was just to take Ann out for a walk and out of the way for a bit as Granny was very set in her ways and didn't expect Liz to be able to do anything right. They enjoyed being together but everyone was getting tired. Even the baby was resting. It was past her due date.

Then came the day when Liz felt lots of contractions and got her father to drive her into the local hospital where she was booked in. Then the contractions stopped, and they were sent home again. Her mother was quite disappointed as she was looking forward to having Ann to herself for ten days.

The second time, Liz's waters broke.

"It has got to be it this time, Dad. The baby really must be on its way. My waters have broken. We had better get to the hospital quickly."

He bundled her into the car for the second time for the short ride to the hospital. The baby was already ten days overdue and everyone said that second babies do not take so long as the first. They hurried to the maternity ward.

After a while, to Liz's great astonishment, they sent her home again.

"Nothing else was happening so they told me I ought to go for a ride on a square wheeled bicycle. I think they were joking, I'm worried in case I get another infection now that the waters have broken."

Her mother could offer no advice since Liz was her one and only.

The third time Liz woke her father up at nearly midnight. He muttered something like, "It had better be this time or it will be a do-it-yourself job."

It nearly was. Fortunately it was a clear run, for Jane made her appearance almost as soon as they reached the hospital.

"Why is it that babies prefer the middle of the night to be born?"

Liz gazed down at her newborn daughter. Her thick dark hair made them think of a little Beatle. "Looks just like her mother," they all said and Liz could hardly wait to write to Will about his new daughter. She was so excited that she couldn't wait until daylight, and the airmail letter was already to post by breakfast-time.

– *"Another girl, and the spitting image of me! Oh Will, your daughter is beautiful! I do love her, and you of course! You missed all the excitement though. I got Dad up in the middle of the night as I was sure she was on the way. Then the pains stopped and I was sent home. The next day my waters broke and he rushed me into hospital again. When I got sent home a second time, he muttered about a DIY job, but when I screamed for him at midnight, he bundled me into the car and we only just got here in time. Good thing it was just a couple of miles, as this time, Jane couldn't wait to make her appearance and we barely got as far as the ward. I wish you were here too. I miss you so much."* –

There were no problems with this baby, but both Liz and her mum were glad of the respite that the stay in hospital gave them so that both mother and grandmother only had one child each to worry about. There was no problem about feeding this little one but Liz needed all the rest she could get to be able to get her established. And before long, it was decided that this hungry baby would not be satisfied with what milk Mum could provide. Liz rested as much as she could, avoided things like swedes that gave the nappies such an awful colour and tried to convince Ann that this baby was not really eating her mummy. Apart from that, she seemed fascinated with her baby sister and insisted on holding her so that a photo could be sent to Daddy.

– *'Ann seems to love the new baby. Long may it last! I think I shall have to ask the midwife about changing to a bottle. I would hate to think that I was starving my newborn, and you can see just how much she gets with a bottle.*

'This time, we have a National Dried Milk baby as Carnation has gone out of fashion. I tried desperately to feed her myself as everyone says that is best, but I am still 'a poor cow' and it had to be the bottle again. Now she is thriving and ever so contented. I'm glad you liked the photo of the two sisters.

'I'm going home again shortly. Time to get on with my own life. It is ever so easy to slip into the role of daughter of the house, but I have two of my own now. Time to be independent. Mum could do with a rest as she won't let me help much. All our love.' –

– *'Home again! No mishaps this time, and I must have the most contented baby ever! It was time we left as Ann has been much more demanding now that she no longer has two doting grandparents pandering to her every whim. She was in serious danger of being spoilt! I do love my two little girls and can't wait for their Daddy to be home to see them!'* –

– *'We are coming down to meet the ship in Plymouth. I have booked us in at Aggie Weston's and Mum and Dad will be going down to Cornwall so they can keep an eye on us on the way. Ann is so looking forward to meeting her Daddy but she will scarcely remember as it has been nearly fifteen months and Jane is already eight months old before you see her for the first time. She is so good. You will love her.'* –

The best laid plans! On the day the ship came home, Liz's sweet and contented baby suddenly turned into a red-faced, crying little horror. She howled her eyes out and was sick everywhere as soon as she met her daddy. Ann was good, though perhaps more interested in the cakes and goodies put out for tea than this brown faced man who was trying to keep her sister quiet.

"I thought you said she was a good baby," he muttered. "I wanted to show them off to all my friends."

"She is, normally. There must be something wrong."

What a home coming!

It was nothing personal, just a really bad case of measles and the doctor advised us to take her home as soon as possible. Fortunately, Mum and Dad called back to Plymouth as Mum had a premonition that something was wrong and they were able to transport the three of us straight away, leaving Will to follow in the mini when he started his leave. Jane was really very ill for a baby, but by the time her dad got home at the weekend her temperature had fallen, and she was getting back to normal but had had a particularly nasty attack.

'After more than a year away, it was a bit like getting to know each other all over again, and the worst thing was probably having to give up driving my car…so that was not too bad. I got no sympathy from my mother as in Dad's day they could be apart for several years at a time and before she had me, she had always to go back to her parents' home.

'Despite the measles, Jane was soon an equal favourite with her sister, and when her sunny nature returned, the whole family settled down to re-learn life together for a while. Will had to get to know Ann all over again as it had been such a gap in her young life, and he also had to meet this new daughter who was quite sunny again now that she was better. Ann had to learn to share her parents since she was no longer the only one, and Jane was soon moving about after her and wanting to join in.

'I didn't know about this as I had always been an only child, and spoilt, I'm sure. I was determined to have more than one, but two was enough. We know the limits of our purse. Will, however, was a second child and has the scars to prove it, so he kept a close eye on them and was usually first on the scene when there was a howl. They had their places, Ann was the first-born spawn and Jane, the baby. There was no problem with rank.'

Will came off the ship and was posted as a trainer at the engineering school, and so he got home almost every night. All the little jobs were done in the house and the garden was perfect.

It is almost like being married to a civilian, thought Liz as birthdays passed and Ann was nearly four, and her shadow tottered around behind her.

Shore-time doesn't last forever, and soon Will was again sent to a new ship based in Plymouth.

'Guess what! Will is going to be an officer!

'He came home with a broad smile to announce that he had got his commission. The exams had taken place ashore after he had persuaded his previous boss to recommend him. He put his name forward in time for his very last chance before he would have been too old to be considered.

'He says you can see the weals across his back where I beat him to make him make the best of himself. He says he would never have done it without his new family to spur him on.

'Apparently, he has done really very well in the exams and will now be going to Greenwich to be converted into an 'officer and a gentleman'. It is an educational as well as a cultural course "to learn how to use the right knives and forks, chat to people of all classes and to charm all ladies from eight to eighty" as he put it. It was also to keep them away from the fleet and to adjust to being a boss rather than a worker. The wardroom is a different world from the various messes he had been through, as he progressed to the top of the 'lower deck.' It could be a bit difficult if he meets any of his old drinking friends, as there is still an element of 'them and us'. It is particularly hard for SD (special duties) officers who have come up the hard way, rather than the direct entrant officers who don't know the difference and have the rank but not nearly as much experience.

'He is especially pleased as it puts him on the same track as Dad who got his commission in wartime.'

The air of command suited him, but he also had the solid practical background missing from many direct entry officers with whom there was always a kind of rivalry, usually friendly, once they had time to appreciate each other's qualities.

New uniforms, gold braid, even a naval sword – he was going up in the world.

"Behind every successful man there is a woman with a big boot," Liz said with a laugh, and he wholeheartedly agreed. Without his family he would never have made the effort.

***

So was it all too much?

How come this shining new Naval officer fell by the wayside?

Well it didn't happen yet, although he couldn't dodge the sociability of the wardroom and the demands on his mess bill.

"We had more money when I was just a Chief," he groaned.

However, he soon settled to his new rank and status.

***

In spring, Liz had her first taste of Naval hirings. Will had to attend the marine engineering college in Plymouth for six months and as it was the last opportunity before Ann started school, the family moved too.

'What a dump! No wonder he packed the mini with bags of coal and all the extension leads he could find! There wasn't room for me and the girls, but fortunately, Mum and Dad went to visit their friends in Cornwall and were able to drop us off.

'The only accommodation available was in part of an old mansion. It is freezing cold and with huge rooms. It is up an outside wooden staircase which is lethal when wet and in the winter it seems to rain all the time. Horizontal rain, too!

'In the sitting room, is a huge fireplace where our bags of coal were soon lost and now it is warmed only by a small electric fire we thought to bring with us and there is no hot water. Our bedroom is big enough to have a ball in, and I have discovered where flies go in the winter for there are hundreds of dead ones in here. This is also the site of the only working electricity point so that is why we had to bring all the extension leads. No wonder Will didn't know how to describe it for me. If this is officers' accommodation, whatever is the rest like?

'We have found out the answer to that. The other family in this mansion have even bigger rooms and a fireplace you could roast an ox in. They are even colder than we are, as a howling gale comes down the chimney. They are hoping to move out soon when a proper quarter becomes available.

'We all huddle up in blankets as soon as we get in, and I have found that the roof leaks in the girls' room and the bed is quite stained. We have moved the furniture around but I don't like it.

'Still, it is only temporary and at least we are all together while we can be. I shall have to do something about hot water though. You can't have much of a bath with a kettle. Good thing Mum and Dad didn't come in to look around. They would have taken us right back home again.

'Desperate measures are called for. We can go swimming every week for the sake of the hot shower afterwards, and my school friend lives about ten miles away so we can visit her and take our towels to scrounge a bath sometimes.

'Today, I was even tempted to dispense with the swim and go straight to the showers. The girls enjoyed the water and splashed around in their armbands. Ann is coming on quite well. I just couldn't face getting submerged in cold water first. I did enjoy the shower though and felt really warm for once. We also make a regular weekly visit to my friend for a bath mid-week and the ring around the bath afterwards is a shameful sight. The first time we went, her dog barked madly when Will came to collect us as, apparently, it has a fear of people in uniform.

'I shall be glad when the spring comes, as the winter rain blows horizontally and we get soaked on the way from the village bus-stop to the old house, and Jane has had to learn to walk as there was too much mud on the drive to be able to use her push-chair. But she is a strong little toddler and tries hard to keep up with her sister.

'Spring has come and it is a different world. It is a very beautiful place we are living in. The grounds of the old manor must have been really something in its hey-day Everything is better now that the sun has come out, apart from the lack of hot water of course. We are able to go up on the moors at the weekend and the girls love that. There is an animal sanctuary nearby that we can visit and Will is teaching them all about the wildlife and the names of plants and teaching me how to scramble up banks and steep hills. We all love the countryside so that is something else we have in common. We only have about another three months together and then he will be off to sea so we are making the most of every minute.

'In summer, we found that there were lots of coves and beaches to visit. I met up with the wife of one of Will's friends who had been on that far away mechs' course. She knew all the best places to visit where you wouldn't be ripped off for car park charges, so I took Will to work and then we went out for the day. We have all got quite brown in this early summer. I shall be quite sad to leave Plymouth just when we were beginning to enjoy ourselves. Will has only a short leave before he joins his new ship so he went home last weekend to open up the house and see the disastrous state of the garden!

'Ann is five today and will start school in September. We went down to the open-air swimming pool at Manadon to celebrate. She is a big girl now, so she cast off her arm bands at the swimming pool to prove that she could do it alone now. How swiftly childhood passes! The only trouble is that I shall be a lot less confident about taking them down to the beach now she has found her independence.'

***

After that last summer, Ann started school about a mile down the road, and Jane was becoming more independent. Getting to school on time was a bit fraught as they never seemed to leave enough time to allow for Jane wanting to walk part of the way

Will had the car, as the ship he had joined was Plymouth based, of course, and the family was back at home. That was always a problem for sailors and their families, and the roads between the two ports were always busy especially at weekends. Soon, he would be at sea again. With the prospect of one girl at school and the other soon of nursery school age, Liz began to look towards the future. It was time she found a new career. What if something were to happen to Will? He was in the services after all and could be posted to anywhere. This time they were heading east again and there was trouble up the Gulf.

Liz had her car back and was able to visit the naval wives for coffee mornings. Several of them were hoping their husbands would leave the Navy now that they had reached the age of 30 and had not got a commission. They would see what civvy street had to offer.

Liz was also able to take the girls up to visit her parents at the weekend and they did love to go to Granny's House. Her Dad was quite impressed with their knowledge of wild flowers and animals.

Liz began to think about what she should do as a new career. She tried one or two ideas that could be based at home but, although they sounded good at first, there was not much money to be made out of them. You met new people which was quite good in the transition between housewife and a real job.

Will was away again so there was always the question of child-care while he was in the Service.

If we had more room, we could perhaps get an au pair and we would be covered while he is away, she thought and began to look at training positions. The probation service sounded interesting, but they threw up their hands in horror at the thought of an au pair to look after the children.

It looks as if I shall have to go in an entirely different direction, Liz thought.

Chapter Nine
Moving On

While Liz was still considering how to get back to a worthwhile career, she received some bad news.

'Will has been 'casevacked' back from the Gulf to the naval hospital in Gosport. He has injured his leg, falling down a ladder, and he has developed a thrombosis which is life threatening. My neighbour babysat for me while I rushed to the hospital to see him. The doctors told him that if the thrombosis gets to the top of the leg, it could kill him. His leg is elevated by a hoist to stop it moving and he has been told to stop smoking or it will definitely kill him. I have brought home all the packets of cigarettes he had with him. I'm so worried; I shall probably smoke the lot myself. What will happen to the girls and me if he dies?

'Fortunately, they have managed to disperse the clot just in time, and he will have some sick leave before he has to go and join the ship again. It has moved on, anyway. He has really been shocked by his vulnerability. Now, he has the girls. It is all so much more vivid.

'We shall really have to talk about my future. I need to consider whether we should move to a larger house as prices seem to be going up daily. I'll see what I can find out.'

Liz took the opportunity to collect a number of leaflets from local estate agents and bring them home as house prices were rising rapidly, and it was a 'move now or never' situation. The accident had happened at a good time from that point of view. A house a few doors away had recently been sold so that gave them some idea of prices. Their bungalow had more than doubled in value since they had bought it. The house near their favourite beach was for sale, but by the time they thought about it they were too late. In a weak moment, Will agreed to put their house on the market, and it was sold to the first viewer. *Drat! We should have asked for more,* they thought. Anyway, that fixed their price range.

'I think I have found a good house in a nearby village. We have put in an offer. We took the girls to see it and their first reaction was, "Now we shall be able to get a dog!" If that is what they want, that's what they will have. There is plenty of room, but they will have to wait until their Dad comes back. There will be lots to do before that.'

There was lots to be arranged before Will had to rejoin his ship. He would not be at home for the completion of the sale so Liz would have to be legally responsible for all that, not to mention the packing-up of the old house and the moving into the new. It was all quite daunting. Finally, moving day came and all was just finished, and Liz was surrounded by boxes when the phone rang. It was Will, sending his love and support even though he couldn't be there. All the girls wanted to know was whether they could have a dog when he came home! The house was just right for a family with a dog.

Naval wives certainly have to be special, moving home, buying new furniture and even giving up the wheel of the car when the master came home! The latter was especially hard as in the new village a car was really essential. It was a long, long walk to the shops.

They had time to settle in, Ann to start a new school, travelling by bus, and Jane to enjoy being the sole object of her mother's attention for a while before Dad came home again to work at the engineering school again, this time as one of the officers.

'He has come home, laden with gifts. He has brought the girls bikes, and having put one together, he is riding round the lawn and flower beds on a decidedly wavering path. The little girl next door told her mother that riding a bike must be very difficult as Ann's Daddy keeps falling off into the rose bushes! He is so happy to be home and likes the new house, though I did get ticked off for buying some red dining chairs without prior approval. Anyway, I like them and they were in a sale! He approves of the big chest freezer, so we can buy in bulk and make some savings on the food bill. There are lots of things he will be able to fix now that he is home.'

First, they had to get a dog. After all, he had promised. So big Rusty came into their lives. A true mongrel and a true friend, who despite his size, suffered being loved and played with by two little girls, taken on long walks by his master and fed by his mistress. A dog who knew where all his priorities were. We all knew that despite all this, he was Will's dog really. "We men have to stick together," he said.

'When Will first went to the RSPCA to get a dog, he came back with a cat because they had no suitable ones available. The cat stayed with us for a couple of days while the doors were shut but at the first opportunity escaped and went to live in the nearby woods. I suppose, I should never have fed her with 'Go Cat'. It was a dog we really wanted so he tried again and came back with this great big mutt.

'I suppose it had to be a male dog to keep the balance right. Will is a bit overwhelmed by a house full of females. I suppose that it was different when they were babies but they are real girls and can wind Daddy round their little fingers. It had to be a big dog too, I couldn't imagine him with a little pooch. This one is big enough to stand up for himself and is a definite 'Heinz' a real mixture, parentage unknown. I am sure he will get a lot of loving from our pair and he looks right following Will, in his wellies, as he goes down by the river for a walk or down to the local pub for a pint at weekends. It gets a bit fraught with the girls sometimes, and I suppose he is glad to get away. This intermittent parenting must be quite difficult. They object to being told what to do and at once. I suppose I have been a bit lenient with them while he was away. But they are only little.

'Now that we have a larger house, it would be possible to have an au pair to look after them when I start a new career, but I sense that Will would not want to share his home with anyone else, particularly a female! I shall have to turn to teaching, I think, as at least I shall have the school holidays. In any case, it was what I wanted to do while I was still at school.

'The nearest teacher training college is in Portsmouth, so I shall have to get in there before the start of the new term in October. Shame they don't offer French, but I can go for geography.

'I got my interview, then came the question, "So you want to be a teacher? Why is that?"'

'That is the question that all job seekers have to beware of. I had to do some very fast thinking to avoid the honest answer of 'For the school holidays'. I must have come up with a reasonable response as I was accepted and offered geography and what was called 'the middle school option' which enabled a teacher to teach either in a junior school or the early years in a secondary school. Thank goodness for a good general education. I may have to cope with all my O-level subjects as well as the A-level ones. The course is for two years and geared towards mature students, mainly mothers who have to juggle their studies with their home responsibilities.

'Jane will have to go to a private school instead of a play group until she is old enough to join Ann in her school. Fortunately, it is on the way to Portsmouth if I follow the back roads, and there is a lady in the village who will look after them both until I get home.

'I thought that getting Ann to school on time was bad enough but getting to college is a nightmare! Not only do I have to get Ann up to the school bus, but then, I have to go in the opposite direction to get Jane to her private school and then on through all the rush hour traffic to get to Portsmouth. I go the back way to avoid as much as I can but I am ready to collapse into my chair when I arrive. Some of the other mothers have an even worse journey. Good thing it is a mature students' course, and we can commiserate with each other over coffee. Some have to rely on buses and trains, at least I have the mini, so I can be a bit more flexible. My new friend has the dickens of a journey, dropping off her son at a nursery in Gosport before she starts to come here. I give her a lift back home and we can chew over some of the lectures in the car. A lot of the course is 'teaching granny to suck eggs' so far as we mums are concerned, but I suppose it has to be included for school leavers and we have only two years instead of three, but some of the psychology takes a lot of swallowing. Some of it is utter nonsense, but we have to pretend it is wonderful just to keep in with the lecturers.'

Their budget would be very stretched for the next couple of years, as in addition to other expenses, they would have to pay the fees to send Jane to the private school until she was old enough to start at the real school. There was a grant, but that would only cover travel and books as there was no time to use the library.

In the time before she started college, Liz tried to earn some more money in part-time work, but it was swallowed up in expenses, as they had to get a family car so that she could run the mini to college. Jane had to be kitted out in her new uniform, pink summer dress and a boater!

Will tried getting the train to work, but the car was really needed. In any case, the dog wouldn't fit in the mini when everyone else was there.

**

The next two years were a bit of a blur. There was, suddenly, so much to do. Liz travelled to college by car after dropping Ann off at the bus-stop for the school bus, taking Jane to the private school on the way and then trying to get to Portsmouth, avoiding the traffic jams and arriving as near to on time as possible. She met another student who was to become a best friend, who had an equally unpleasant morning routine but was glad of a lift back in the afternoon. She was doing history. The deal was that Liz would find the route and Jen would get them there on time. The last lecture was always terminated by a shuffling as mothers prepared for the mad rush to pick up their own children after school.

College itself was a joy as they had the chance to become students again and to get around in jeans and sloppy jumpers, putting the world to rights over coffee and arguing about what the lecturers had really meant. You could tell that they had never brought up children as they waffled on about child development and psychology. Still they had to read the books and pretend they agreed in order to get the grades.

Liz thought of the university time she had missed out on, but then she would never have found herself there, married to a sailor and with two lovely daughters.

She also had a typist as that was one of the skills that Will had learned in the Navy, and though he didn't understand a word, he typed up her final thesis for her. Anyway, her understanding of his technical skills was pretty grim and she should never be let loose with a screwdriver.

Then it was summer and the last holidays, before starting teaching. Liz had decided to go for the secondary school option, as she didn't want to teach children the same age as her own and bring her frustrations home.

During her course, Liz had gone to several schools for teaching practice. Some of them were an eye-opener for a girl from a small country town, and she could scarcely believe some of the family backgrounds. An opportunity had come up in the nearby town of Fareham, so she was lucky to have found a place so close.

They went on holiday to Norfolk, camping in a tent borrowed from the Navy. It was an unfamiliar area to Liz with broad beautiful sands and the cold North Sea. In fact, at one point, the girls were swimming and suddenly a third head appeared next to them. Will was down the beach like a flash to keep them safe, as an encounter with a seal was not recommended. Rusty opened a bleary eye and wondered what the fuss was all about. So much for their guard dog.

Although she would be teaching fairly near to home, it was still a logistical nightmare until Liz found that a new family had moved into her road and her new friend Meg had a son a couple of months younger than Jane. School buses and after-school problems were solved, as Meg also had a younger daughter.

Will just couldn't believe the differences between education in the Navy which is a disciplined service and what went on in schools where discipline was honoured in the breach. Liz's school was actually quite good for discipline as it had been a boys' school and they had just brought in their first year of comprehensive girls as well. They still kept the slipper for the boys, but there was a softening of the attitudes with the advent of the girls.

She was teaching geography as a main subject, but also some French and English. The teaching was enjoyable, though some of the reference books were a bit ancient and since she was only teaching the lower years, discipline was not really a problem. Some of the older boys were disgruntled, as the school leaving age had been raised to 16 and at the end of the day some escaped through the windows instead of attending the last tutor period. Will couldn't believe his eyes when he saw this, as he was waiting for Liz one day.

Nor was he impressed by the load of marking that she had to bring home each evening. That was just the teacher's lot. You couldn't avoid it as during lesson time you had to keep an eye out for the troublemakers who were ready to stir things up the moment a teacher was distracted. There was no opportunity to mark books.

"I thought we would have time together in the evenings," he grumbled and went out with the dog.

Liz was beginning to develop migraines and, at first, she put it down to stress, but she became aware that it might have a different cause.

'Migraine again, and I really don't want to be off sick, as I know what a problem it is when someone has to take over your classes. I have been feeling lousy lately, and Will is really fed up as I seem to have a period three weeks out of four. I feel like death warmed up. I thought the migraines would stop when I came off the pill and Will had a vasectomy, as I was so worried. But he says he needn't have bothered as he can't get near me anyway. The doctor had suggested a D&C, so I hope the waiting list is not too long. Will is due for another ship soon, so this time is precious.'

Liz had nearly finished her probationary year which meant qualified teacher status; she didn't want to have it interrupted by sick leave.

Life was about to change for all the family.

"I've been offered a married-accompanied appointment in Hong Kong starting in August," Will announced.

A two-year married-accompanied tour in Hong Kong was a real dream for a family like theirs and just at the right time too as Liz would have finished her first year and the girls were still at junior school. Hong Kong had to be the most exciting place for a geographer and with all the time Will had spent in the Far East, he was looking forward to showing it all to his family. They were able to pack up everything at the end of term, sell the car (the mini had finally expired that year) and let the house.

Even the dog was catered for as Will's brother had left the Navy and agreed to look after him.

Chapter Ten
Living in Hong Kong
(Extracts from Liz's Diary)

Wow! The heat hit us as soon as we got off the plane. Everybody has been very helpful though, as we are in a temporary flat for a week until the proper one becomes available. I can't complain about the floor space as we have about as much as in the bungalow. The neighbours are quiet though. We back on to a Chinese cemetery. We are a bit isolated apparently, but who cares! All I want to do is sleep. The flight was pretty long and we didn't get much sleep on the way. We even stopped in the middle of the night to refuel, and as we sat in a café we were surrounded by the croaking of frogs. The heat was like a warm, wet blanket.

We met a nice couple on the plane, an army sergeant and his Chinese wife, Chris and Chris. The wife was very much looking forward to going home. I don't expect we shall see much of them as we move in different circles, and the army and navy do not seem to mix much socially or only rarely.

Ann didn't have a good flight as her ears were hurting every time we changed altitude.

I was not very amused when we got off the plane and one of the officers who came to meet us told Will that the ship was going back to UK in eight months' time. So much for our two years out here and all the plans we have made! We needn't have sold the car or let the house for only a few months. They could at least have let us know before we did all that.

The girls are shouting that there is a monster in their room. The chit-chat lizard on their walls is growing into a giant every time they open their eyes. If you believe them! I expect that we shall get used to all the wildlife in time. Anyway, chit-chats keep the flies away and I am all for that!

First Naval function tonight. There is a cocktail party on board and we are to be picked up at six. It's a good thing I packed a long dress in my luggage as our main baggage won't be here for a couple of weeks even though we sent it in advance. The girls have settled now at night so the babysitter should not have a problem. Will has got one of his lads to do the honours.

It seems even hotter today than it was before. Thunder weather has never been my favourite as I get headaches.

I disgraced myself tonight. I have never fainted in my life before. We were standing on deck under the awning. There were fairy lights under the awning and flashes in the sky. It was quite a storm brewing. All of a sudden, I felt woozy. We went over to the railing to try to get some air but it was like breathing a warm fog. I handed Will my glass and muttered "I'm going." Before he realised what was happening, there I was stretched out on the deck, looking like one of those ghosts from the cemetery behind our flat.

I wasn't there long before someone brought a chair and a glass of water. Soon, we took a taxi home. The new engineer's wife had really let herself down. I was fairly told off for making such a show of myself but then Will admitted that the humidity was exceptional that evening. It is pouring with rain now and already feels much better. I have also learned another thing. No nylon clothes in the tropics. We shall all have to go shopping for cotton clothes. Thank goodness for markets. I'm no good at haggling though, as everything seems cheap to me. The shopkeepers don't respect you without a haggle, so I shall have to learn.

Our new home is gorgeous. We are on the fifth floor of a block of flats overlooking the racecourse at Happy Valley on Hong Kong island. We have a huge lounge and dining room combined, two vast bedrooms, two large bath and shower rooms, a kitchen and, across a kind of balcony, a little room for an amah or maid. Apparently most families employ a maid, but there is nothing to do until I get a job, and that won't be for a bit as I need to explore first. The windows of the lounge overlook a big concreted over area of the hillside which is a water catchment area. Water is always needed on the Island and when there is a storm, it is funnelled into storage areas like the one below our terrace. I'm pleased that we are not overlooked by hundreds of windows, as the tallest flats seem very close together. We are not too far up the hill, and there are some steps leading down to one of the important markets. It is easy to walk down but we need a bus back up to the end of the terrace or better still, a taxi. There are lots of taxis and they are relatively cheap for us to use, and Will has always got around in taxis when he has been here. I want to explore the buses, mini-buses and trams that the Chinese use, as I'm sure they are far cheaper and fun to be on. Since we shall not be here as long as we had been expecting, there are lots of places and shops to visit, and I want to have some money to buy things while we are here.

The supermarkets stock everything we could expect at home, but there are also extras in the special Chinese food sections, including bottled snake among other things, and of course a lot of American foods that we wouldn't normally see. The markets are great for really fresh vegetables and fruit and the meat is practically killed while you wait. You really have to wash the fruit and veg when you get home as the favourite fertiliser is night-soil, or human dung! It is also easy and cheap to eat out and when Will comes home we usually try some of the restaurants, English, Chinese or, the girls' favourite, MacDonald's where you have to stand around tables to eat your beef burgers. Apparently, Hong Kong has the first MacDonald's outside America, so it is a privilege. I prefer to eat in more comfort.

Most of our day is spent in or around the swimming pool at the Naval base and Will meets us there after work. The girls are getting really good at swimming and will soon be going in for their bronze survival awards. They will have to start school soon and there is a bus from the end of the terrace that takes them to the junior school on the army base. I shall then have to start job hunting, as I shall miss them even if they only work half days and finish at 2 pm.

I took my doctor's advice and have to go into the British Forces' Hospital for a D&C. There is no waiting list here.

I have found a job in a Chinese secondary school, teaching English to senior pupils. It covers five and a half days a week, but unlike the Chinese teachers, I only have to go in when I have a lesson scheduled. I could hardly cover for other classes since I don't speak the language. Sadly, there is no point in learning to speak Chinese, as we have to go back before too long. There is also a staff room where I can do my marking, so I shall not have to bring work home, that makes a change. The school runs two sessions a day, for morning pupils and for afternoon pupils and they alternate on Saturday mornings, so I only have two lessons a session that is four a day weekdays. The girls are pleased that I have got a job. Now, we can have an amah to do the housework and to be there for them if I am at work and they are not. We have also bought a television set. Many programmes are in English and the cartoons are the vital part of the programming.

What a difference between the Chinese and English pupils! These really want to learn, well nearly all of them. There is a tannoy system in the classrooms for announcements. For the first week, the headmaster made the effort to make announcements in English as well as Chinese so that I knew what was going on, but he is back to Chinese now and my pupils have to translate for me! Most of them are very shy about speaking, but very polite. After my attempt at the register at the beginning of the lesson, I assure them that their spoken English is better than my Chinese pronunciation. It gives me a thrill when I am out shopping and someone says, "Good Morning, Missy." I feel as if I am part of the community. I may not recognise them if I don't teach them, but of course I am recognised by all the school. They are incredibly smart in their uniforms. The boys all in whites, and the girls in tartan skirts, white blouses and ties.

Ah Hay, our amah, is a wonder woman. She is ever so good with the girls, and there is no problem if I am late back. They are deep into children's television anyway. She seems to spend all her day washing and ironing. All our clothes are beautifully kept and she has a lot more patience than I have ever had. She is also happy to babysit if we go out in the evening, so I don't have to worry about that.

I just wish that the Navy didn't party on a Friday night when I have to get up for school on a Saturday morning. It is not that I drink a lot, it is the sleep that I miss. I have never been a morning person. One of the attractions of this posting was the night life that goes with it so I must not complain. There are not only Navy functions but also top acts that come to the big hotels as you are out for dinner. We have to make the most of everything while the ship is in port. They are going on patrol on Monday and will be away for three weeks. We shall miss Will, but I am going to take the girls exploring by bus and tram during the weekend and there is always the pool to visit during the week.

When he comes back we shall have such a lot to show him. We have been all over the Island and have found markets full of clothes. The nice thing about Hong Kong is that we find the people very friendly and we feel safe exploring even on our own. Although the trams are so crowded, there is no problem as we strap-hang along with the rest and their baskets. On Sunday, though we did feel a bit out of place as we went down to a beach which was so crowded that we didn't feel very welcome. I can understand why most of the expats have access to banyan boats to take them off to swim and picnic on some of the nearby islands. Next weekend, we shall take a ferry to one of the islands where it should be a bit less crowded.

There was a dance to celebrate their return to port and Will's boss was as drunk as a lord. Everyone noticed and Will was very scathing, but I can see how it happens. He was mixing it a bit as normally both men and women drink the local beer which is fairly innocuous, almost like lemonade. Lemonade or coke get very sickly after a while so the beer is easier to drink. Spirits can be cheap but you need the mixers which are much more expensive, so normally we stick to the local beer for a cooling drink. In fact, we buy beer with the groceries. It is cheaper than bottled water. There is always a can to hand in the heat and it is easy to lose track of how many you drink. At school, I have got used to drinking Chinese tea. There is always some going, and we have mugs with little caps to keep it warm and fly proof when you have to go for a lesson.

We took Will for a tram ride. It was his first ever and we could see a lot from the top seats. We caught the tram at the terminus and went all the way to the end of the line. Near the end there was a fishing village. It was a collection of wooden huts on stilts over the sea. From the tram, we thought that we could see some flames. When we got out, there was a pall of smoke rising with flames leaping high into the air. The huts would go up like tinder what with all the nets and stored oil for the boats and cookers and all the dry old timbers. It was quite frightening how quickly it took hold. I hope nobody was killed, but it was certainly the end of that village. We read about it in the paper the next day. It rather spoilt our pleasure in our day out.

Another scare today. We were out on a banyan boat. They hold about 20 officers and their families and are really floating gin palaces, well Pimms palaces (the mixture of fruit juice, booze and fruit salad) for the adults and copious fizzy drinks for the kids. They also serve a good salad lunch and soup as it is coming towards autumn now. We swim off the boat or go inshore to the pretty beaches on the more remote islands. We try to find a beach where no other boats are anchored and enjoy the day diving off the boat, swimming or snorkelling. The girls had gone inshore to go snorkelling with their Dad. They were better than I was as I'm sure my nose is the wrong shape and I nearly drown myself.

Anyway, we were anchored about 300 yards off shore. It was not a good swimming day for me so I was still on the boat and the three were ashore. The girls have their bronze medals now and are normally quite safe. Ann decided to swim back on her own. About two-thirds of the way back, she must have swum through a chain of jelly beans (jelly fish eggs) and got stung. It is painful but not normally dangerous. However, she panicked and might have drowned. I dived in and did the fastest 100 yards of my life, but Will, with his flippers, got there first all the way from shore. He was worried about her, but of course, once on the boat and after a bonus bottle of coke, she was fine again. It is good to have such backup from the other parent, as with kids, you never know what they are going to do next!

I have never been so cold in my life! We may be in the tropics but trust us to come to Hong Kong when it has the first snow in 21 years. All of a sudden there was a cold snap and we went from summer dresses to lots of pullovers, and I have even bought a padded jacket like the Chinese wear.

In our flat, we sit around with blankets around us, hunched over the television with all its Christmas adverts. The shops are full of decorations and I really must get some, but I don't feel very cheerful when I am so cold. The trouble is that the houses are geared towards feeling cool when it is too hot and they are not draught proof. There is a positive gale in the classroom at school because there is a gap under the door and the windows don't close. If you are outside, it is quite beautiful to go for a walk as the skies are clear and sunny, really pleasant after the heat and humidity. The ship has gone away again, down to Manila. They must have heard the weather forecast.

For Christmas, we invited Chris and Chris. They live over in Kowloon, and we had not had a chance to meet them since we arrived. By then, we had an artificial tree and lots of decorations. We really went mad as the shops were full of them, but we shall never see anything like this again. It might not look like Christmas outside, but it does indoors.

After the cold snap that made the Chinese so excited, it is really quite pleasant again and I am down to one jumper or even just a blouse. In fact on New Year's Day, the girls even went in for a swim. Only briefly though.

We were over in Repulse Bay for a dance when there was a typhoon warning. That was the end of our evening out as all the sailors had to go back to the ship as it was going out to sea for safety. That left all the women and children at home to batten down the doors and windows and stay inside until it was safe to go outside again. The Chinese junks had been streaming back to harbour for several days to take refuge in the typhoon shelter. Now the storm had taken a turn towards us, and it was expected to be a really good blow. We made sure we had bottled water and food to keep us going for a week and we had to watch the television to follow the instructions and to know just what was happening. It was all new to me of course, but to the old hands it was just one of the hazards of living out there. These things pass.

They were quite right but at the height of the storm things were very hairy. All sorts of junk was being blown about outside, anything that was not safely battened down, sheets of corrugated iron from roofs and lots of other lethal objects. I thought of some of those flimsy huts we had seen on the other side of the island. There was no school of course. The children's programmes were interrupted by storm warnings. Then came the rain, in sheets. It rushed down the water

75

catchment area at the back of us and flooded the lower levels. I was glad we were living on a hill.

When it was all over, we could go out again. The girls went back to school and I waded to mine as public transport still wasn't running. It was not too far to go over the hill and I enjoyed the different route. It was amazing to see that all the Chinese children turned up in their sparkling whites despite everything.

A few days later, the ship returned. Naval wives have to be pretty self-sufficient as it is up to them to keep the family going when their men are away.

There was a ladies' night on board to make up for the dance that was interrupted by the typhoon. We were all looking forward to it. That day an Australian naval ship came in to port and the officers of Will's ship were all invited on board for drinks. Our evening was scheduled for 7:30.

Five o'clock came, and no Will. Six o'clock. At 6:30 he arrived, drunk as a skunk. I was flaming! The taxi was due at seven.

He was hauled under the cold shower just as he was, uniform and all (good thing it was whites), until he could make sense of the world again. At seven o'clock we were both ready. He was still blue, slightly shaky and contrite. He was not the only one. All of the husbands seemed to have had the same treatment and one couldn't make it even then. The ladies had a good evening but the men were only able to push their dinners round the plate. I hope I never see him like that again.

I have had my call for surgery. It is to be a hysterectomy and I need to be off work for six weeks. I have managed to get another Naval wife to take over my classes and, fortunately, the ship is not scheduled to be going anywhere so Will and Ah Hay will be alright with the girls. I have to admit to being a bit scared as this is major surgery, losing my womb and all that implies. Mind you, after all the troubles I have had and Will's snip, all it really means is losing a bloody nuisance every month, (and I mean that, literally!) Things have got to be better after this is done.

Well that is all over, then. It was a bit more than expected, what with all the adhesions from the infection after Ann was born and, apparently, I gave everyone a scare when I was in intensive care. Surely, I didn't look that frightening. Anyway, so long as nobody makes me laugh too much, it can only get better from now on. I feel as weak as a kitten though and can't carry anything. I'm glad I don't have to return to work for a month. The girls are so untidy, dropping things just as they take them off. I didn't appreciate how much extra work they gave Ah Hay. I can't pick things up for them so they will just have to learn to help themselves. We shall not have a maid when we get home.

We have got a function to go to with Chris and Chris in a week or two, and I have had a new silk dress made to show off my new slim figure. My weight is less than I have ever been since I was about ten. Some of it is from the operation but a lot from living in the tropics with all that fresh fruit available. With the heat you don't need a lot of bulk. I wish I could believe that I won't put on weight when I get home again, but it is nice for a little while to feel all glamorous, especially after that kind of operation.

The ship is going home in about five weeks' time, but because they are going round 'the pretty way' it will take several months and the children will be able to see out their school year. And so shall I, once I am back.

We have decided to send Ann to boarding school next year. A lot of her friends are going to one or another and I shall be glad that she will be in a more stable environment than the secondary comprehensives I have met and heard about. She has had this hearing problem where she tunes out of lessons. I think that smaller classes will be a help. That is another problem we were able to have looked at while we were out here. They picked it up at school and she had her hearing tested. With my family history it was very worthwhile. She may grow out of it or on the other hand the deafness may return later. At present, it seems to be linked to adolescence when all sorts of growth rates get out of synch. It just shows up as intermittent deafness.

The ship is off on some kind of a farewell courtesy visit. It is due to be replaced by small ones only. Their main job will be to patrol and stop too many mainland Chinese trying to get to live in Hong Kong.

The girls and I are left alone for a while, and we have given Ah Hay a short holiday to make up for all the time she had to put in while I was in hospital. I really shall have to get the girls a lot more used to clearing up for themselves, long before they get home. They have picked up some really bad habits and I certainly can't wait on them. I managed to walk down the steps to the market the other day, but there was no way I could have walked back. I shall have to get in some serious swimming when I am allowed again.

Down in the market, the girls hovered around the fish stall where the fish are presented for sale with their hearts still beating to show that they are fresh. The girls are fascinated. There are also live fish swimming around in tubs. Sometimes, these are taken home in a kind of raffia parcel still wriggling as it hangs from the fingers of its new purchaser. The storekeeper is equally fascinated by the English girls, especially Ann with her blonde curly hair. Before I could stop him, he had presented them with a live fish, in its raffia parcel, to take home as a pet! It will never survive. Good thing we were going home in a taxi.

Will went up to the water catchment area with the big green plastic dustbin and got some water to keep it in and we are feeding it breadcrumbs. Contrary to all expectations, it appears to be happy with that and growing fast. It has been named 'Goldie'.

Would you believe it! Our last night out together and my chance to wear my new silk dress and what happens? The girls were playing with some other kids down below the flat, and I was getting ready for our night out. A white-faced Ann appeared in my looking glass and muttered, "Jane has fallen off some roller-skates." After my shaky experiments on roller skates, I had refused to buy any on health and safety grounds, but of course that didn't account for borrowing from friends. We went down to see. She had not just fallen down but had broken her arm badly. That was quite obvious. There was nothing for it but a visit to the hospital.

We called a taxi and Will stayed to comfort Ann, who seemed to think it was all her fault for letting her sister try the skates. I had to stay with Jane for hours as she had had some chocolate before going out to play so they couldn't give her an anaesthetic until later and it was going to need surgery as she had well and truly broken her arm. She didn't do things by half. It was a really nasty fracture and warranted a couple of days in hospital before a long time in plaster.

So that was Will's last few days before the ship sailed for home. All three of his girls had been patients in the hospital at one time or another. When he went to visit Jane in hospital he decided to donate 'Goldie' to the fish pond there as if we couldn't take care of ourselves what chance for a goldfish in a dustbin?

I must say that we felt a bit stranded when the ship set sail. We had come out to be together for two years and less than eight months and several mishaps later we were on our own as the ship left Hong Kong loaded to the gunnels with souvenirs. Will was even using a rattan peacock chair to sit on in his cabin. It was the only way to get it home intact.

However, once we got used to the situation, we managed very well, shopping and eating in the places we had visited as a family, though perhaps not as much. In fact, one day the Chinese butcher in the market called out to me "Why you no buy from me anymore, Missy?" When I explained that my husband had sailed away, he was sorry for me and invited me to share a meal with him and his friends. Very nice thought.

There were very few invitations to go on the Sunday banyan boats so the girls and I explored the other beaches we could get to by ferry and became very proficient on buses and trams. Shopping excursions were important as time was getting short, not to mention money, as we knew that there were many things we would never be able to see or purchase again. I was back at school, but I learned to take shortcuts that taxis would never use. A short walk would save a lot of time and expense. We often had baked beans on toast for a meal in the evenings, but that too was a treat. I found that some of the Chinese shops had food a lot cheaper than the supermarkets we used to use and there were also mysterious objects in bottles that we didn't want to look at too closely. How do you cook snake anyway?

Today, Jane had her plaster off. It has been six long weeks of hot weather. She has not complained, but it made my heart grieve to see her swimming in the pool with one arm held straight up in the air to keep the plaster dry. I failed my silver survival medal, because I couldn't climb out of the pool at the side, but the day after she had her plaster removed both she and Ann passed theirs. All that one handed swimming paid off for Jane. She must be really tough. I can't wait to let her father know. He will be really proud of her. Of them both. He used to swim for the Navy.

They must be half way home by now and we only have a month until the end of term.

That's it. The boxes are packed and ready to go. I've spent just about everything I've earned. I just want to buy some earrings before I go. Having ears pierced in the tropics is a bit dodgy so I am waiting for the last day. I finish school next week. It has been a good experience, and I shall miss my classes. It will soon be exams and I hope they will benefit from having me teach them. I have been asked to invigilate for some of the exams held in big examination centres. Apparently, they all have to wear name badges with photos on so that you can check that it is the real pupil who is sitting the exam. Sounds a good scheme to me.

We are due to move out of the flat and into a hotel for the last night or so before we go. That means we can give the flat a real blitz. I remember how strict they were when we moved out of that awful hiring in Plymouth and even tried to charge us for water stains where the roof had leaked. I am looking forward to getting back to our own home now. I wish that we had been out here longer as I really love the place, though it is not the same without Will around. I miss him, and I bet he misses us!

I don't believe it! How could so much happen to one family? Here I am in hospital again.

I left the girls with one of the other mothers and went off to get my ears pierced and buy some jade earrings I had been eyeing for a while. On the way back, I slipped on a dodgy bit of pavement and sat there looking at the bone sticking out of my leg. Like Jane's arm there was no doubt. It was well and truly broken. As I sat there, the Chinese walked around me and I could have been on the pavement for ever as I certainly couldn't move. A little sports car drew up. It was a young Ghurka officer, who picked me up, leg stuck over the side of the car and prepared to take me off to the hospital.

We were supposed to be flying home the next day. Fat chance! I got him to take me to the pool and go in and find the girls and their minder. She agreed to take them back to the hotel and wait while they rang Chris and Chris. With all the other families from the ship due to fly back the following morning they were the only people that we knew who would be staying there and would have room for a couple of lodgers until other plans could be made.

Two very subdued girls came in to see me today. Chris is doing her best to look after them but really has no idea about children. My heart bleeds for them. I shall be stuck here for several weeks as despite having the fracture pinned, you can't fly home with a plaster on, for fear that the leg will swell up. Will got the message when the ship reached Gibraltar. He must be going out of his mind with worry. He was expecting us to be safely at home by now and instead of that we are all still stuck out here. They are trying to get passports for the girls as they were included on mine. Once they have their own passports, they can fly home to Granny's House. The plane comes in to Brize Norton and that is not far. Will can meet them there and take them to my parents. What an awful muddle! I don't know when I shall be able to leave here. I know I was tired at the end of term but I wasn't expecting all this bed rest.

Well, they've gone, poor little souls. All that way in the care of another Naval mum they didn't even know. Still, their daddy will be there to meet them when they get off the plane. Now, I can concentrate on getting better. There is a chance that I can get casevacked home, still in plaster, if they can get me on a medical flight. Apparently, it is the most comfortable way to travel on a stretcher all the way. In the meantime, I shall go up to the women's ward to see if I can cheer them up with my tale of woe. Stand by to hold in your stitches!

Chapter Eleven
Home Again

The stay in Hong Kong had a lot of repercussions that were not immediately recognised.

The first was, probably, the habit of drinking bottled beer instead of any other cold drinks or even tea or coffee. It seemed as weak as water but it was insidious. In a hot humid country, a cold drink was always to hand.

The visit of the Australian ship, the Vampire demonstrated how dangerous was the Naval wardroom culture of drinking spirits to excess and then trying to pretend it hadn't happened.

The accident-prone family must have caused deep anxiety for Will as he was helpless to prevent it at the critical points when he was at sea. They coped without him (with difficulty), but it must have been a blow to his protective instincts.

There was more to come.

On the plus side, he had a great experience as the engineer on a frigate, making the sole voyage back to England the 'pretty way' while the family completed the school year.

After Liz got casevacked back, she was allowed to go home, although her leg was still in plaster, and she was on crutches.

'Home again! It didn't take long for me to talk my way out of hospital after we landed at Brize, especially as it was not far from Granny's House where Will had taken the girls. We stayed for a few days but now we are back home. The grass is ten feet high as nobody cares for the garden when you are renting and goodness knows what they did to the settee. We shall soon get things sorted.

'Well, first we shall have to get a new car, an automatic, so I can drive while I still have the plaster. They put screws into the ankle so it will be quite strong when it is all finished, but when they take off the plaster it will feel strange. It is not going to be good for some time. In the meanwhile, the ship is still in Chatham until it is de-commissioned, and I have crutches so I won't be going far in a hurry.

'Rusty has been returned. Will's brother brought him back last weekend, probably with a sigh of relief. Rusty seems keen to revisit all his old haunts, though I can't take him far. He was really pleased to see all his family again.

'Disaster! The dog escaped again. Leaped right over the six-foot gate and went off to visit his lady-friend about a mile away. I managed to get him back twice, but last night he didn't come home and we went out to look for him. We found him lying at the side of the road, dead. He had forgotten that roads are for cars, not dogs. I hope nobody was hurt in the vehicle.

'Will will be devastated when I break the news when he comes home tonight. He really loved that dog.

'It was really not a good weekend. Will had to go and get his dog from the ditch as he was too heavy for me to move. Then he buried him in the garden under the apple tree and went off down the pub. We haven't dared go near him. He was in such a black mood. After all the worry of me breaking my leg, the girls flying home on their own, this is the last thing I could have wished to happen. On Sunday, he went off back to Chatham looking very bleak.

'What a summer! All the disasters in Hong Kong seem to have followed us home and now it is nearly time for Ann to go off to boarding school. Already, I am dreading that. It seemed the natural thing to decide when all her friends in Hong Kong were planning the same, but now…at least it is the year when everyone will be going to different schools.

'She looks very solemn in her new uniform, a bit lost in her blazer, but I wanted one that would last for several years. I never want to sew on another name-tape. You wouldn't believe how many there were. We have nearly packed her trunk, and we shall be taking her to school next week. In a way, I wish it was Jane who was going as she seems more outgoing and is already bored back at her primary school. At least, I don't have to worry about Ann's hearing. Will took her to an appointment at Southampton University and they say it may be only temporary, this hearing loss.

'When we leave her, she will not be allowed home for a whole six weeks. It is supposed to help new pupils settle in all right. Jane will really miss her, and so shall I.

'I get my plaster off next week too. I expect the leg will be all pale and hairy. The screws will hold the bones and they will have to be removed in about six months. I shall be glad to get rid of these crutches. Despite all that weight I lost, there is still a lot of me to carry around on crutches but they couldn't use a walking plaster since it was really my ankle I mashed up. I shall be glad when I am a bit more mobile.

'It was awful seeing her go into that school alone, though the staff seemed very nice. They must have a lot of Service children and some parents are a lot more than 80 miles away. We didn't talk much on the way home. The school itself is like a manor house but the dorms in another old building were a bit spartan and four or five to a room.

'The good news is that Will has got a new post, lecturing at the Fire School in Portsmouth, so he will be home at nights at a reasonable hour give or take the traffic jams, of course. It will give me a chance to look for a new job even though the term has started.

'Jane is at the junior school now and can go on the bus. She is repeating much of the work they did last year and is bored stiff. I expected a problem when she transferred from private to primary school but once again she is back-pedalling. I did ask if she might be put up a year, but no chance in a state school. She also seems so much more grown-up than her friends.

'I have been offered a supply post at the local secondary school. Apparently, a teacher left after only a week or two. It is to cover maths and science, not my favourite subjects. The deputy head was also a geography teacher and he thought it would be no problem for me, so I shall give it a go. Geography seems to have disappeared off the curriculum at least in the lower school.

'Ann will be home for the same half term as we have. Jane and I have seen an advertisement for some Labrador cross puppies not far from Ann's school, so when we go to collect her we can give Will a special belated birthday present. He turned 40 just after Rusty was killed and he had always dreaded that birthday, so it was not the time to celebrate. Let us hope that a puppy will cheer him up a bit.

'Our family has grown by two. At first, he said he didn't want another dog as his own dog was killed, but we persuaded him to go and look. We were just in time as there were only two puppies left without homes. There was this dozy dog-pup, the runt of the litter, and his sister who had an eye problem but now seemed to be taking care of him. Well, we couldn't leave her, could we? They are very sweet and very small but they have very large paws. Mum was a Labrador and Dad was the red setter from down at the farm. They are a bit redder than most Labradors and have long hairy tails. Will says they belong to the girls and not him as his dog was killed. I'm sure he will come round in time. He has called them Rusty Two and Copper. Since they were the last of the litter, they are a bit older than usual and by the end of the week have become quite used to us all.

'Wow! This timetable is tough! You would never believe what a crowd of first-years are like in a laboratory. No wonder the other teacher left! At least, I have two years experience even if not in that environment and the bits and pieces of other lessons are fun. The staff is nice which is always essential.

'I'm worried about Will. He seems to be having a rough time too, but of course never tells me about it. Perhaps it is work or perhaps something else. He seems to be having mini panic attacks and has to leave the classroom until he composes himself. I can't believe it is lack of experience as he could run circles round most young schoolies in this particular field as he has had so much time at sea. Perhaps, it is like me and driving. I have been much more aware of dangers since I had the girls. Whatever it is, he doesn't really like the job and he seems to be drinking even more. He comes home and takes the dogs out and then goes down to the pub until the meal I have been getting has gone cold. Jane and I keep out of his way as much as possible just to keep the peace. Anyway, as soon as she is in bed, I have lots of marking to do. I usually sit in the lounge with him to keep him company until he drops off to sleep. By the time I have finished, he has gone to bed and is snoring enough to make the walls shake.

'He came home tonight in a terrible state of 'nerves' and couldn't wait to get down the pub. Even the dogs had a very short walk.

'It is strange when you realise that the strong man that you married is becoming less and less able to cope with the demands made on him. Perhaps it is the demands of the job, lecturing on safety and fire-control at sea. Perhaps the very nature of the subject brings home dangers that may be ignored when you are young, free and single. As a parent, you are faced with your own vulnerability and the consequences for your family. The helplessness he must have felt when we had all those problems in the last weeks in Hong Kong can't have helped either.

'There are times when Will has come home still shaking with the pressures of the day. I don't think it is just the pressure of teaching, after all, he has had several posts involving new-entrants and teaching basic engineering skills and he would be the first to admit that sailors are a lot more disciplined than the youngsters I am called upon to teach. But then, if it gets too bad, I can look for another job and that option is not open to him. He is not very well impressed by his current boss and seems to be doing a lot of extra for him.

'I don't think that drinking so much is doing him a scrap of good. It is supposed to affect the brain and panic attacks and claustrophobia are aspects of mental illness. He even gets claustrophobia shopping in the precinct and it is not because I spend so much money. I tease him that all men get claustrophobia when their wives go near the shops, but I really am concerned. There is no way he will go to a doctor as that would be an admission of failure and the Navy doesn't do that.

'Having to enter confined and smoke-filled spaces as part of the courses must try him to the limit, and he won't expect his students to do what he cannot himself. At least, it is not for real as it would be in a crisis situation on a ship. I'd hate it myself.

'It is bad enough dashing off to the pub the moment it opens. The neighbours could set their clocks by him. Now, when he comes back he deliberately avoids me. He goes outside and sits on the stump of the old fir tree with a tumbler full of homemade wine. He looks so lonely sitting there. I wish he would tell me what the matter is. The dogs are there, one on either side. Occasionally, he pats one of them. They are very loyal. They wait all day for him to get home, but their walks are getting shorter and shorter. Whatever has to be done gets done in that brief space between 5:15 and six o'clock opening time. The garden doesn't get the attention it used to. He used to have a scorched earth policy and now the weeds are as bad as when I am looking after it.

'I really don't know what to do or say without being accused of nagging. He surely must realise that this is doing him no good at all.

'I shall be glad when he gets another job. It must be nearly time. We thought the fire school would be good as it was a change and a challenge and enabled him to have some time at home, but it seems to have been a real disaster. The only plus has been the barbeques they laid on in the summer. They know all about lighting fires as well as putting them out!

'My last few days as a supply teacher! I had a term of maths and science then another doing all sorts of lessons at the local school. No sign of geography though. I even had a tutor group of first years. They really worried me as there was such a sexual tension. The girls were devastated when they lost boyfriends and there was a lot of bitchiness. I had a word with the head of year. They aren't children anymore and they can't handle their emotions like adults should. I'm worried about some of them. Then for the summer term, I had a job in Southampton as an English teacher in a school with a broad ethnic mix. I suppose my teaching in Hong Kong helped me to get that post. Anyway, I applied for a permanent job now my ankle has settled. I am to teach French and European Studies in a new school in Gosport. I'm looking forward to that.

'We shall also be able to send Jane off to join her sister at boarding school. I shall miss her but she has been quite lonely, living in a village without Ann and her friends. I must admit that Will and I have not been good company for ourselves, let alone for her. She will do well in the more formal situation at that school too. They actually tried a free-choice timetable, for juniors, and don't talk to me about Fletcher maths! "Why do I have to do the same sum different ways, when I got it the first time, Mum?"

'I expect they will put her up a year after a few weeks when they recognise her ability, and I shall be pleased to see her out of the state system, the way it is going. Ann has settled in happily now, though she did put us through it by bursting into tears as we approached the school after a weekend at home and making us think we were cruel parents. Then she forgot something and when we went back five minutes after we had dropped her, she was happily playing with her friends.

'I have started at my new school. We only have years one, two and three so far and I have a tutor group in year two. The new young teachers who joined last year have been promoted to subject heads and head of year and the school is run on a shoestring with most of the children using worksheets instead of textbooks. Geography is part of an amorphous mass that includes history, R.E., English and Personal Development under the heading of Humanities. I have found that all children are taught in mixed ability groups, including for French and that the European Studies is for those who can't tackle a foreign language. There are some who have a shaky grip on English, let alone French. With a young and inexperienced staff and experimental lessons, not to mention mixed groups, I suppose that worksheets are a necessity and you just need to be a few pages ahead of the pupils. However, some of the French is inaccurate i.e. full of mistakes, and I am going to have to tackle my head of department about that. Thank goodness my pair are at boarding school. Just imagine them in a class of 30 of all abilities! Actually, the kids are not too bad considering some of their backgrounds and I have a really good tutor group.

'Will is still at the fire school, but seems to be less stressed there. Had a change of boss so that might be something. I am settling in well in my school but you have to have eyes in the back of your head with some of the groups. It is a bit better to have organised them in smaller groups still mixed, just like an infant class, for sometimes those who have got the hang of it can help the others I can't be everywhere all at once. I look back nostalgically to the well-behaved Chinese pupils sitting in rows. Thank goodness our girls are having a more formal education.

'I have decided to take some of my pupils on a trip at Whitsun. It will be to Germany and the kind of coach tour experience that they might otherwise never have. There will be no pressure to speak the language, but I believe that travelling abroad opens the mind and we can call it European Studies! Our girls don't have a break at the same time so that is fortunate for once. We only overlap some of the holidays and they enjoy going to Granny's House to get spoilt.

'It was an interesting trip and provided a few eye-openers. One evening, there was a complaint about the noise from our hotel and the police were called. It wasn't our group, but it was surprising how everyone materialised from wherever they had been and assured me that, "It's alright, Miss. We won't let you down." Obviously, more important than tricking teachers was showing solidarity before the police! I only found one boy with his hair wet from being sobered up under the tap by his fellows but no doubt there were other bottles around.

'The biggest problem was with my own health. A few weeks earlier, I had caught the German measles that was going around and one of the side effects was joint problems. My knees were terribly swollen on the coach trip, and I had difficulty climbing stairs. On the way back, some of the kids locked themselves out of their hotel room and 'so as not to worry me' they climbed from the adjoining windowsill into their own room. Four stories up! I turned grey on the spot when they told me later.

'A few weeks after we got back, I went for an interview for a year-head job in another school but came second. I really need better qualifications before the next opportunity comes up. Nothing more this year. Generally, I like this school, with a certain notable exception, so I am not too put out and my headmaster has put me forward for a term's counselling course in September and I have also applied for an In-service degree course in Winchester, so for one term at least I shall be a full-time student again.'

***

The drinking didn't ease though, and Liz had to be quick if she wanted to go with him and the dogs on their pre-pub walks. Apart from that, it was pretty lonely for Liz without the girls. You may be surrounded by people at school, but there is nobody to hold a conversation with. Liz considered going down the pub too sometimes, but she really couldn't see the point of paying for expensive drinks when there was nobody to talk to there either. It wasn't a sociable activity. She still had her good neighbour down the road when she was at her wits end and needed someone to have a moan to, and apart from that her hobby was work. Even the garden was beginning to look neglected, though as the summer came in, Liz hoped that, perhaps, Will would notice and get back to what used to be his favourite hobby.

They decided to take their holiday walking the Pennine Way with the dogs, each day on a different stretch and camping at night. Away from his normal routine, Will was quite happy and taught the girls some of his country lore and lifted the dogs over styles and laughed as they peered over every stone wall to look for the sheep (they continued to do this all their lives). He got tired with the need to do the job of erecting and taking down the tent every day for of course the others were only allowed to assist with the easy bits, and there was no call for any alcohol to help him sleep. It was a good holiday.

For Liz, the job was always a challenge, not the pupils or the subjects but the boss. It was a new school, and run on a shoestring, so there were trendy ideas and no textbooks. Mixed ability classes for all and trying to teach a foreign language to such a class! Liz was not happy with the quality of the worksheets offered to the pupils and that it was alright to ignore mistakes both on the worksheets and by the pupils. It might work in some subjects but not in languages. The European studies which had seemed so interesting a concept, combining geography with languages was also a problem as it was only taught to those who couldn't cope with French and the geography element had been cribbed out of sixth form textbooks. Liz offered to re-design the course. Well, that kept her busy!

'My head of department is the end! Not only is her French worse than mine, and I haven't even been to university, but she insists on using worksheets with mistakes in the grammar. She makes me flaming mad! These children have doubtful enough English let alone being exposed to bad French. When I brought it to her attention, she told me it didn't need to be accurate!

What is more, I am not allowed to correct mistakes in red ink, in case it puts the pupils off. We have to do the marking in green biro. I ask you! I wish I could have a moan about it to Will, but he doesn't want to know about my problems at school. I suppose he has enough with his own job.'

The pupils were alright. They were in quite a poor area and their home conditions made one amazed at how they managed. Every day, she started with a clean slate and didn't carry over the problems of the day before. Eventually, they built up quite a bond. It was especially obvious when they went on that school trip Liz had arranged, the coach trip to Germany.

Despite the trials of teaching during the day, Liz was looking forward to further studying, as a change from marking books. Anything to get some real grown-up conversation back into her life! There would be the full-time course during the first term in addition to two evenings a week at college.

The autumn was going to be busy.

Both girls were well settled at school and when their holidays were different, they were always welcome at Granny's House. The dogs could be coped with.

Liz had just started being a full-time student again when Will came home with some great news. Despite all his troubles at the fire school, he had got promoted again and would have a higher rank than his father-in-law achieved. That was his ambition! He had been offered a plum job too. He was to be the engineer officer of a survey ship in the Antarctic. Only an SD officer could really fulfil this role, as it required lots of practical experience as the ship was an independent command, with only one engine and going to uncharted waters in the icy Antarctic. The ship is an ice-breaker and they would be going right through the pack ice. He was so excited! He had to fly south to relieve the current engineer in South America, another area that was new to him, and he would be with the ship until it came home for refit in May and then away again in the Autumn. Liz was less excited at thinking of him in such dangerous waters, but she was really happy that he had found something to look forward to. He never drank at sea either. It might make her studies easier over the next years, but she really didn't fancy rattling around at home with only the dogs for company. However, she had known that would come when they sent the girls off to school. She would feel less guilty about spending all her time in books, essays and marking when there was only herself to worry about. There were the dogs too, of course, and during that first term she would have to come back from Winchester on two days to feed them and walk them before going back for the evening session.

'It is such great news that Will has got his promotion and now the challenge of this new ship. It could be just what he needs to break the bad habits and get back to being the man I love and am so proud of. He doesn't drink while he is on a ship and with all that responsibility it will be such a challenge. Of course I shall miss him, but I shall write a bit every day like we used to, and there are satellite phones now that they can use occasionally. The dogs just won't be a bother and my friend from the training college is also on the degree course and will drive me in the evening as she needs lots of practice in a car.'

Chapter Twelve
Alone Again

Liz was enjoying her counselling course though she sometimes thought that all the participants needed their own counselling. She wasn't the only one whose marriage was in crisis, and there were others with all sorts of problems. The various strategies they learned were not only geared towards school, and they did one to one counselling of each other as well as group sessions. The group sessions were a bit strange, as they all sat round in a circle, waiting to see who would break the silence. Liz was a bit concerned about what she might say if she got going, but there were plenty of others with more urgent needs. She was envious of the lecturer who said that at the end of a bad day he went home to cuddle his wife. It seemed such a long time since she and Will had been able to share like that.

At the end of October, Will left to fly to Argentina to join his new ship. Apparently, they did a lot of socialising in South America to 'fly the flag' as well as the survey work proper in the ice-fields with only the penguins for company. There are a lot of families of English or Scottish extraction in Argentina, and they are invited to their homes, and they also made contacts in the local navies.

Liz managed to juggle her courses, even coming back to walk the dogs on the evenings. She found that many on the counselling course were considering using it as a lever to leave teaching, but several were using it for their own therapy and to have a break from the chalk face. Liz did a special interesting presentation on epilepsy, following a television programme. She learned a lot, and it gave an insight on how diseases could affect not only the sufferer but also their families and their actions and reactions. She tried hard to think of the person apart from the presenting problem. That certainly applied to drinking.

As teachers, you might never know the personal demons that your pupils are fighting. It is a wonder that some of them are not a whole lot more trouble.

'I have just been for my usual Sunday afternoon walk along the beach. The dogs need a really long walk at the weekend after being tied up so much. I don't get to take them far in the evenings so they are ready for some real exercise come rain or fine. I don't really mind the rain as it gives me an opportunity to have a good cry and nobody can notice. I can always blame the wind in my eyes. Sundays, I consider a family day, so I can't inflict myself on my friends and, sometimes, I feel so dreadfully lonely. There, I have admitted it. It all comes back to that counselling course and when the tutor said he could cuddle his wife if he had had a bad day. I have been bottling up my feelings for long enough, and you have to let go now and again before putting on that brave face again. I realise that I have been unhappy and lonely for years, not just since Will has gone down south. It is not just the physical distance we have been apart, it was the same last year when he was at home. I just wish we could get back to the closeness we had when we were first married. We could lock ourselves away in our home, and there we were as a family, poor but contented. I suppose things move on, and I really miss the girls too, but they are better off at school and away from the system where I am working. It is a bit better now, as we have a new German teacher who shares my views on accuracy, so that is a help. Perhaps, everything will begin to look up.

'I still write a bit daily, though it is sometimes hard to avoid things at school. I expect that Will is also lonely at times, even though he has a whole wardroom of companions. It is not as if you can choose who you work with. I feel a bit disloyal when I only consider how I feel without somebody to talk to but then I just bury myself in my books. The counselling course was full of interesting aspects and some of the teachers were looking for applications outside of teaching itself. I really enjoyed the careers counselling bit and the child psychologist's input showed how quickly a child could pick up a label they didn't really deserve and then try live up to it. In my school, I met the daughter of the lady who escorted the girls back from Hong Kong, and she started giving me a spiel straight out of one of the textbooks. It was to the effect that 'My parents really don't understand me'. So I translated it for her and told her that that's how a lot of teenagers felt, no need to feel unusual because she had been told the long words for it. I hope it did her some good and helped to pay back her mother for her kindness.'

They went to Granny's House for Christmas. It was really convenient that Liz's father could collect them when they had longer holidays than the state schools and they were always welcome there. They even had to take the dogs now as there was nobody else to look after them. Liz's Mum was terrified of them at first because they were so big, but they soon proved to be real softies and lived in the back porch so everyone got on alright. Liz decided that in the New Year she would see that the girls got more exeat weekends.

'I am looking forward to the weekend when the girls are coming home. I collect them Saturday noon, go home, do their washing and then get them back for Sunday tea-time. The time is very short, but precious and I shall have somebody to talk to. Teaching is a very solitary profession although you are with so many pupils in a classroom. You don't really have time for a conversation. It is not like in an office where you can spare a minute or two to chat to a colleague. I'm lucky if I even get to the staff room for break times.

'We have something planned for Easter though. My new German colleague has organised a trip to her home town on the river Elbe for a week at Easter and, of course, I volunteered to go too. In fact, I shall be able to take the girls as well since Ann is the same age as most of the pupils and will fit in well. After boarding school, they are able to get on with other pupils I'm sure. I just hope they don't gang up on me or tell too many tales, both ways! We shall be staying in a youth hostel there and, apparently, you can look across the River to the Eastern Zone.

'Poor Ann. She got halfway across the German Plain and went down with hay fever for the first time. I suppose it was all the tree pollen. Anyway, we got some drops from the chemist for her, and it is getting better. At least, she can breathe more easily. I was really worried as on a school trip you are responsible for your pupils, and I was very torn because it was my daughter who was in difficulties. Still, after that everyone got on very well. My girls joined the others in the 'us against the teachers' band. Not that any of them are badly behaved, they are aware of how lucky they are to be on such a trip, just like last year. In fact, we were pretty concerned when we found a boy with some pornographic playing cards. I blew my top and confiscated them, muttering things like 'loss of childhood'. My number one daughter told me to keep my cool. They had seen much worse than those at school! Why are we paying so much money for her education? I must have led a very sheltered childhood.'

On the in-service degree course, there were a lot of senior teachers and primary heads. After a long day at school, their boredom threshold is not very high and the lecturers had to keep on their toes. Head teachers are very good at making paper aeroplanes. The lecturers had to keep real as the experienced teachers had been there, seen that, several times round. It gave Liz hope that some of the crazy ideas in teaching might just be a swing of the pendulum and that it would turn back before long as they were found to be unworkable. As they travelled together to give Jen some practice in driving, it was also good to be able to discuss their course and experiences in schools. Jen was in primary schools. Liz was convinced that she had made the right choice in going into secondary schools, though there were pros and cons on both sides.

Although she was desperately lonely now that both Will and the girls were away, at least there was no more treading on eggs, and she could work when she wanted, even stay behind and visit the library on that first term, a student pleasure she had never been able to experience before. It was a breathing space for her marriage and when she received letters, they were friendly and loving as before. This sea time had been a reprieve instead of building up into an explosion and saying things she might have regretted.

(Liz's diary)

Sometimes, I wonder how much of our marriage problem is my fault.

I really have been tied up in this business of making teaching work for me, and I'm frustrated by still being on the bottom rung when some incompetents, I could mention, are doing very nicely, thank you. Perhaps, I really do have too big an opinion of myself. On the other hand, since my German friend joined this school we have both agreed about the inaccuracies on the worksheets and they are going to get some textbooks and do something about setting for languages so the good ones are not bored stiff and the poorer ones have something at a speed they can cope with. Now, there are more teachers available I suppose these ideas are easier, but I have also used the experiences of other more established teachers on the B.Ed. Course to add weight to my arguments.

I don't think that my problems with the hysterectomy, before and afterwards, did a lot to cement our bonds either. I used to find love-making a way to feel really close, then with all the problems...and now he isn't even here...

I really find it hard to cope with the sheer loneliness. I may have been a bit of a loner before I met Will but that was up to me, and I could always go home for the weekend if I needed a bit of company and some home-cooked food. Now, I am supposed to be the centre of my own family and home. I ought to be more self-sufficient but with the girls at school and Will away until the summer all I have is the dogs and you can't have much of a conversation with them, no matter how much they try. At least, I now have someone to talk to at school, at least in passing.

The ship arrives back in Chatham in May. I shall not be able to get there and anyway Will will have to stay on board until he has set up the refit. He will not get back to Portsmouth until Friday. I'm really looking forward to seeing him. It has been long but eventful six months. I hope that life will be easier than it was before he went away. The break will have done us good from his letters he seems to have got a lot out of this trip. I am looking forward to seeing his photos.

Chapter Thirteen
Fresh Start

Big trouble! I should have met Will at the ferry, but there was a panic at school and I couldn't get away on time. He stamped his way up to the school and was waiting by the car. It is not like an ordinary job where you finish at a set time but this is difficult to predict and I don't like asking for concessions. Anyway, by the time we got home and the dogs had given him an ecstatic welcome I think I was forgiven. It is really good to have him home again if only week-ending. Now that the ship is in refit, all the other officers are on leave but the engineers have to keep an eye on things so there is no peace for Will. A solitary ship down among the ice-fields can't afford to have a breakdown on their one engine or they will end up like their namesake, stuck in the ice. Anyway, I am still busy at school. We are nearly at the end of the year with exams and report time coming up and that is always fraught.

I have just got my notice in and I shall be leaving at the end of term. One of my fellow students on the B.Ed. course is head of languages in another local school and he has offered me a job teaching French. They teach it properly there, too. I am really looking forward to it and will be with colleagues I admire. I have really done my best where I am and the pupils appreciate it. I shall miss them. Well, some of them!

Oh dear! Will is back to his old routine of the pub run again. That didn't take long, but at least he has lots to do to catch up in the garden. I tried to do my best, but once the grass started growing again, it was a struggle. Starting the mower has always been a problem for me. You don't marry an engineer and expect to deal with recalcitrant machinery!

Will won't have a row with me even when I get really exasperated. He just goes quiet, goes off and grabs a bottle. I just burst into tears. I know I shouldn't really as there is nothing men like less, but I am so frustrated. There is no point in getting a meal ready if he isn't here. Then that is wrong. Or, if I get it, it will be cold before he gets in, and that is wrong again. He has been so spoilt on this trip!

Why does he always turn to the bottle? It would be better to talk about what is wrong, not go off and sulk on his stump. Is there some magic genie in the bottle? Doesn't he realise how much I missed him and how lonely I was here on my own. Surely, he knows how much I love him? Does he really love the bottle more than me? I can't fight that. I would fight off another woman but he is here in body if not in spirit. I suppose he will be out there until bedtime now. I might as well get on with some work. He will go in later and shake the house with his snores. Again. There is not even any comfort in our bed.

I frightened myself tonight. I got halfway home from school and couldn't remember the journey at all. I sat in the car and just shook for at least ten minutes. What with the tensions at home as well… Thank goodness it is nearly the end of term. I could really do with a holiday.

I am going to take the girls to Brittany with my mini and a tent. Will is still involved in this refit and won't have leave until later when we shall probably take the old caravan off to Dorset as usual. I am a bit concerned about taking the girls on my own, but we should have fun together.

You will never believe it! We met Jen and her family in Quiberon at the supermarket. They have a caravan nearby. I bet she doesn't sleep with a carving knife under her pillow! We are invited over for supper tonight. Her husband is great with my girls and teases them and treats them like his own family, just as I do their pair. It makes me a bit envious to see such a happy relaxed family. Jen's husband left the navy a couple of years ago so he can see both sides of the problem. He has a local job and can see how the children are growing up as well as understand that the Navy owns you 24/7 and you have to do what is needed. I wish Will could get back to the happy relationship he had with the girls when they were small. They are very wary these days and say he treats them like his sailors and thinks more of the dogs than he does of his daughters. I am sure it is not true, but I can see where they get the idea. Perhaps, dogs just don't play record players at full blast!

Well, I enjoyed the holiday but I am pretty glad to be back home in a real bed. Must be getting old! It has been good to read something that isn't a text book too! Jen and I were able to laze on the beach while her husband took all the kids off for more energetic activities.

I have caught up with the neighbours a bit as the girls have been looking up all their old friends. Some they were in primary school with, and some who live further down the road. Haven't they all grown! It is a pretty good village in the summer when everybody is about but in the winter everyone is indoors and it is more isolated.

Heard some shocking news. When I was at the local secondary school, and I was really worried about that tutor group, well, one of the girls lived near us, and I have just heard that she killed herself with her father's shotgun, over an upset with a boyfriend. That is horrible. I can scarcely believe it and she can't have been more than 14.

Our family holiday in the caravan was not too bad as the weather was good and the sea not too cold. Will and the girls were snorkelling round the rocks but I generally stayed on the pebbles with the dogs. I haven't been too keen on British waters since we went to Hong Kong. The trip to Antarctica seems to have made Will hardy again. The water around Durdle Door is clear enough, not like in the Solent, where I have bathed once or twice in desperation when it was just too hot.

The only complaint was that ours was the oldest caravan on the site, so it is about time we got another one. This one will be good as a garden shed as we still haven't replaced the one that was crushed when I was still training to teach. Gosh, that seems such a long time ago!

The old caravan has been painted green and named 'Kermit's' and so is a retreat for the girls and their friends when they don't want to come indoors. Will and I have regained some companionship, taking long walks along the beach or through the woods as the girls and the dogs range on ahead, and the garden is standing to attention so the end of the holidays has been a good time for us all.

I am so pleased that I changed schools. I have a pretty fair timetable and even one top set, which does make a change. It is nearly all French too and book-based, not the dreaded worksheets. I am quite looking forward to this term.

The pupils are taught according to their ability and you don't have to keep worrying that you are losing some, as the others leap ahead. The discipline is better too and they are in awe of some of the heads of year or of department.

Will is looking forward to going south again. "It is autumn and time to follow the birds," he says. The refit went well because he was on top of things. He is enjoying this ship and looking the better for it. I have even been taught how to make the mower go, besides swearing at it, and I have a suitable spanner to restart the mini when the starter motor packs in in wet weather.

He brought back some stunning photos of ice and rock formations last year. It must be very beautiful but far too cold for me. I wonder what the photos will be this year.

I'm glad that I didn't write him a 'Dear John' letter last year, though I was sorely tempted and the frost wasn't only on the hedgerows. He seems to have made more of an effort since the holiday with the girls. Life has been more pleasant all the way round.

This is Ann's O-level year, and we need to keep her well supported.

I shall soon be heavily into college again. It is only one evening a week this year, separated into primary and secondary groups, so I shall not see much of Jen. Good thing she can now drive herself to Winchester. My colleagues at school seem very nice and helpful. Nowhere near the same tensions as in the last school. Was it only last term? It seems ages ago.

***

The girls also went back to school. Their parents were no longer intimidated by the moans and groans as they approached the school as they knew they would soon be off with their friends. Ann was in her O-level year and the brief holidays in France and Germany had given her confidence, so she was beginning to work hard and not have so many disagreements with her house-mistress. She found it easy to be led astray and then was so honest that she was always caught out. It wasn't easy for her to have a younger sister who found schoolwork easy, but they seemed to have reached a balance.

Then, it was time for Will's ship to leave again. Liz was not looking forward to being on her own again. She had hated the distance that was between them, not only in miles but also in feelings. She had hated his absence, but it was only his absence that had enabled her to cope with the problems at school, that and throwing herself into her studies. Now she had turned her life around and changed what she could, and the next year would see the degree course finished. Perhaps it was the absences that had allowed her mother to cope as well, for there must have been times when living with Dad was not easy. Liz was a strong person. She would not go running home with her problems, but a good weep now and then worked wonders.

Since she had changed schools, it was surprising how much easier the teaching was with colleagues to consult and give support. She felt that at least she had her career and would, at a pinch, be able to provide for herself and the girls if anything happened to Will. He had never denied them anything and was always a good provider, money-wise. It was just his presence that was denied to them when he had his dark periods. He loved them, she was sure, but there was still that something else that had changed him.

The girls had got closer to him during the holidays again, and they would sometimes write letters to him. Liz made a point of writing something every day and sending it when it made a decent sized letter. He was even able to phone on occasion, but it all depended on where they were.

Liz didn't see so much of Jen now unless she paid her a visit. They had a year to complete an ordinary degree or an extra one for honours.

Ann had certainly settled down to work now. Her mock exams had left something to be desired but she was determined to show her French teacher that she would pass, despite his doubts. There was a school trip to France at Easter and Liz decided to take the girls. Jane, however preferred to visit her friend's home. Liz agreed and then found out that the friend lived in the Caribbean! Fortunately, Liz's father came up trumps and provided the money for the trip as a Christmas present for it was an experience not to be missed.

They went up to her parents for Christmas and then on up north to Will's younger brother who had left the Navy and taken a pub, so there was room for all of them and Liz, who didn't bother with drinking for a very good reason, would do the chauffeuring for all the family for New Year. Liz very much liked her in-laws, but was still wary of the snow ploughs kept in threes! Her sister-in-law had got used to this strange southern family and despite Will's absence, they had a very good holiday.

'We are off to France for Easter, and I shall be driving a minibus. It is a school exchange trip so the pupils will be living with families, but Ann and I have a caravan. The other teachers are camping and have all the gear, not like lying on the floor like we did last year!

'Ann has improved her French, living with all those teachers, she is determined to pass and show her French master that she can do it, so there! Driving a minibus full of pupils was an interesting experience and a half. However, away from their own territory, the English pupils were pretty good, unlike the French pupils who came in exchange. The biggest complaint about staying in French homes was the strangeness of the food, as if they normally ate in gourmet restaurants! I really laughed when I overheard one telling another that she couldn't wait to go down the Chinese and get some real food again!

'May and the ship is home again. I have really missed Will. Weekends are always the worst, and I have shed many a tear as I have walked the dogs along the beach. I hope things will be happier this time. I have heard a lot about high living in Argentina where the ship's company had many invites from families with British connections. He was even offered the chance to ride a horse on one of the ranches. It will be back to basics here!

'I didn't attempt to meet him this time. I got in enough hot water last year. It is not that I don't love him, but I can hardly leave a class of 30 pupils just to meet a train or a ferry or even a ship. We arrived home at about the same time and he took the dogs out while I cooked supper. He has lots of photos of penguins this year. They are mainly dots on icebergs. He is still enthusiastic about the ice but pretty pleased to be back home as well. We both went down to the pub for a drink as we have not yet got the big car ready for use. No studying tonight!

'It didn't take long for him to get back into the routine with the neighbours setting their clocks by him. I suppose it is difficult with him on leave and me still working. He is out on the stump, looking like a black Tuesday. I'm not going to make a fuss of him. I have got work to do. He will be returning to Chatham on Sunday night as the refit has to go ahead.'

***

She just let him get on with it. She couldn't afford to get all upset at the drinking for drinking's sake and she certainly didn't want to join him in that.

It was soon time for the refit to start and Will was back to Chatham, commuting at weekends. They did manage to buy a new caravan and have a few days together in the New Forest at half term. They planned to use it for the summer holiday as well.

Liz managed to keep weekends free of school work when Will came home even though there was an awful lot of assignments and school work to be done during the week. They managed to go up and visit her parents a couple of weekends, Will and his father-in-law made a very similar couple as they went along to the local pub. Liz and her mum muttered together.

Liz went to pick up the girls at the end of term. After exams, Ann had been to camp with the cadet force.

When Liz went to pick her up, she was slumped on the pavement with her luggage around her, absolutely exhausted, having completed obstacle courses, orienteering and self-catering on army rations. "I'm sure it has done me good, Mum," she muttered as she fell asleep as soon as she got in the car.

Jane would start her O-levels the following year, and she was not going to join the cadet force. She still had a week to go until the end of term and then they would be all together at least at weekends. Liz was looking forward to having Ann at home again while she did her sixth form studies.

***

Ann has finished her exams and is not going back to school. She has decided to go to a local sixth form college and stay at home this year. I shall be glad of her company. I am going to do the third year of the B.Ed. course to get an honours degree. It is mainly independent work for a dissertation. It will keep me busy while Ann gets on with her studies.

This summer Will has agreed to come with us on holiday to the South of France with the new caravan. I'm glad about that as when I took it to the New Forest at Whitsun I hadn't a clue about reversing. OK, I know the theory about turning the wheel in the opposite direction, but my mind tells me that is illogical. I have booked a campsite and will be quite happy to navigate. Perhaps, we shall get some sun then as it has been a rotten summer so far. I've got a good route worked out with lots of places to see on the way. I am really looking forward to it!

***

The refit was not doing well. There were suggestions that the ship would be replaced after the next trip south, as it was old for an ice-breaker, and Will had to fight to ensure that all the repairs and replacements he deemed necessary were carried out. After all, it was his responsibility to keep her going once they set off, and with only one engine, albeit a massive one, he didn't want to be at the mercy of the Southern Ocean.

'Would you believe it! The refit has hit a critical point and he cannot be spared. So we three are off alone. Again. I just hope I don't have to back it anywhere as that will be interesting! Ann will have to navigate even though she says she can't read maps. What kind of a geography teacher has she had?

'I am really disappointed, but there is nothing to be done, apparently, so we three will just have to have a good holiday on our own. I shall have to drive all the way and probably navigate as well. The dogs will be in kennels and we shall be all right. Damn the Navy!

'We had an overnight stop in a lay-by and then got to the campsite. They didn't say in the brochure that it is near a paper-mill. An awful smell. Still we got some other campers to help us manhandle the van into position. That's me for a fortnight! No more driving! Some of the villages and towns were very pretty but tricky to get through and finding a parking place for this rig is difficult, particularly, when you can't reverse. I just followed the sailor's instructions on the ferry. Still, I saw quite a lot as we passed through. The beach here is sandy and glorious, and we are camped in a woodland site so it should be all good.

'I rang home to leave a message to say that we had arrived and guess what? Will was at home. Apparently, he had solved the problem and got his leave after all. I said he could come down by train and join us, but he has already got the dogs out of kennels and prefers to stay with them. Stuff him then! We shall have a good time anyway!

'It means that I shall not get any rest, as I shall be constantly on duty. It is a lovely beach but, apparently, with dangerous currents and the girls go far out of sight. There is also a nudist beach nearby and that is the safest bit but Jane said that when the waves knocked her down and dragged her under, she didn't know what to grab hold of! Bless! I just have to wait and pray. They are both good swimmers but with a dumping sea you never know. They are pretty sensible, but I wish there were two of us so that one could watch the bags and the other go with them. Single parenthood means a lot of trusting to luck. We shall manage, but I am not impressed.'

"Can you cite dogs for divorce?" she said. Liz was not well-pleased.

The weather was beautiful and the sands stretched for miles. Liz sat with their belongings as the girls went off to swim. She realised just how hard it had been for her mother when she wandered off to swim as mother could only watch helpless as she couldn't even swim. The girls disappeared in search of the sea while she was stuck with all the beach stuff. It was a dumping sea too and quite dangerous.

"And there he is playing with the dogs and getting drunk again, no doubt! He could have made the effort. Other fathers would!" she said.

After their time on the beach and in the sea, it was time to retrace their steps. Their friends helped them to swing the caravan around and they headed north again. They had made the most of their holiday and had had a lot of good times, perhaps even more fun than if Will had been there.

'Result time and Ann has done very well, considering. And, she passed her French to spite her teacher! Now she will be able to do what she wants at college. Pity about maths, though, she will have to have another go. It will be good to have her at home while the ship goes South again – for the last time. Yes, they are going to withdraw it after this trip so Will stays on until the end. See you in May!

'We have finally got the builders to give us a start date for the extension. Two teenagers take up a lot more room – both bedrooms and living space. The builders are going to start in November, but I reckon we shall be lucky if it is finished by the time that Will gets back home again. Ann and I will have to make do in the rooms that will not be touched and just heat those. That will be the front bedroom and the dining room. It will be quite an upheaval and great when it is done but it would drive Will mad as he is so tidy and can't stand things out of place.

'I think I am going to enjoy this year.

'I was right about that. One daughter is good company and we have her friends around after college and all put the world to rights around the kitchen table. Ann enjoys college and the social life that goes with it. She has got herself a job in the pub on Sunday lunchtimes, doing the cooking. This is a talent she has never displayed before, but then I don't have a deep-fat fryer and I don't pay her either. She has to throw her clothes in the washer and have a shower the moment she comes in to get rid of the smell. It doesn't encourage me to eat there!

'She says that Will doesn't have any real friends at the pub even though he spends so much time there when he is at home. I suppose that is part of Navy life – always coming and going with acquaintances rather than friends.

'It will soon be time for the ship to sail for Antarctica again, for the last time. I shall not be sorry to see them go as fathers and teenage daughters don't mix very well. There always seems to be a tension. He can't bear her coming home late, though he is rarely awake when she does get in. They are usually in a big group of locals I have known since they were quite young, but I suppose in his own way he worries about her. I hope the college work is getting done, but I too get told off for interfering. I suppose it is the freedom of being away from the strict rules of the boarding school, though I seem to remember that after the O-levels, we seemed to find the first year sixth a quieter time. We did have to stay in school all day but now they seem to have only half a timetable. It just encourages them to take time out. I have to realise that she is nearly an adult and certainly not freeze her out as her Dad sometimes does. Men! They are certainly different from women!

'Well, now we can settle down for six months while the ship follows the sun south. It will be the last trip for Will as well as the ship as it is being retired, and he would have had to leave, anyway, after three trips. He does seem to enjoy this ship, though he had to fight hard to get a proper refit and stop them from cutting corners. I wonder what kind of photos he will bring back this time?'

Chapter Fourteen
The Third Trip South

Will was looking forward to going to Antarctica again, and as they had decided to replace the ship, he would be there for the full deployment, until May.

The builders came in November, laid the foundation and then it snowed. The nature of the work meant that the kitchen would be out of action, only a microwave, a kettle and water from the cloakroom. No central heating, only an electric fire. It was just like being in Plymouth again but without the swimming pool.

Liz and Ann didn't mind as they curled up in the dining room, working on their knees as there wasn't room for the table.

Liz was right, she did enjoy the company of her teenage daughter, and also of the friends who called round after college, sitting over coffee and putting the world to rights. Ann was enjoying college and all the social life that went with it. There was one lecturer who should have known better since she was a Naval wife, but she made fun of Ann for having been to private school. Liz said a few unkind words about her.

She could only hope to set a good example. It was difficult to treat her daughter as a fairly responsible adult, and Will would never have managed it. She made sure that home was a place Ann would feel her friends welcome, so that she could vet them! After all that time at boarding school, Liz and Ann needed to make the transition from child and concerned parent to a real friendship and trust.

The builders were a friendly pair and seemed to get on with the work honestly. It was very difficult leaving them in the house when everyone was out at work, except the dogs, and they were nervous wrecks.

It was a relief to go to her parents and meet Jane there as home cooking and warmth were most welcome.

In the spring, Liz received a phone call from Will using a new satellite link. They only had a few minutes to talk, but he said that their programme had been changed and that instead of making their way home the ship had to turn back as there was trouble in the Falkland Islands. Apparently, Argentina had laid claim to the islands when the ship had turned towards home and there was no longer a Naval presence in Antarctica. They were going back to fly the flag and show that the islands were not deserted by UK. There was precious little else they could do, as it was a survey ship, not a warship and had no armament, but did carry a helicopter. Liz wasn't perturbed by this call, as she was sure there would be more information when she got a letter a bit later.

At Easter, Liz took both girls to France with the school trip. They had a large gite booked for all the teachers and their families and the pupils would be with host families again. Liz was looking forward to the break from the building work and everything. She had not received a letter from Will, but there had been another mysterious phone call telling her not to believe everything she heard. Will said he was alright but couldn't explain. The link was only a few seconds. It was lucky that he caught her before they went to France.

The parents were most strange when we got back to the school last night, she thought.

'They all seemed to be treating me with kid gloves and expressing sympathy. Of course, while we were away we didn't bother with the news. Apparently, there had been a bulletin to say that Will's ship had been sunk by enemy action. I don't believe it. I am sure I would have felt something if he had been killed. There must be some mistake. In his message Will said, "Don't believe all you hear." So I am sticking with that. It has really upset the girls though. I just hope that brief message was true. There is certainly something up though and they are sending a task force down to the Falklands to sort it out. Until they get it together, Will's ship is the only one there and it is only a survey ship. I hope they have a plan.

'I was right. We had another brief phone call to say they are alright and trying to keep out of danger. There are enemy ships searching for them so they will have to stay in hiding until the task force arrives. While they were in South Georgia investigating a landing of Argentinian troops, the Falkland Islands were invaded by a much bigger force. Winter is coming so only an icebreaker can go in the southern waters. It must be a rotten feeling skulking about in the ice-fields, knowing that there are warships out to get you if you don't hit an iceberg first. Thank goodness for short phone messages and satellite phones. We would have been worried to death otherwise. We shall be glued to the television news from now on.

'The news is all of war and of ships being bombed. Ann and I watch every bulletin. I am sure that Jane must too at school. It is doubly hard for her, not having the same support. We will go and see her at the weekend.

'Mum is having a problem with my dad. He has suddenly been taken ill with hepatitis, and she is nursing him at home. I shall have to go up there too at the weekend. One thing for sure, he will not be a patient patient. His life time of heavy drinking has caught up with him and as it is self-inflicted he will have no sympathy with himself and that will make it so difficult to accept help. The timing couldn't be worse, as we are having enough to worry about with the war and Will and what is happening down there.'

There were a couple more satellite phone calls to let the family know what was happening to Will. They had set up a ship repair facility in South Georgia where there were lots of materials available at the old whaling station. Will's early training in make-do-and-mend and seeing what he could find around was put to good use. He and his team had the expertise and they carried some spares and equipment, as they had to go it alone most of the time and were used to effecting repairs. They used some of the sheets of steel and nuts and bolts they found at the whaling station to keep a number of ships running. It must have been an awesome responsibility. They had thought that they might have been sent home when the main force arrived as they were almost out of food and had sent the helicopter to shoot some reindeer that were loose in South Georgia.

Just imagine, trapped in the Antarctic winter and running out of food!

They started back towards the north but were directed to a supply ship and then were down there for the duration.

There was also some news of a battle with a submarine, but information about this was pretty thin. Will had said earlier that the marines they had taken on board had used his grindstone to sharpen their weapons. He was essentially a man of peace, his task was to see that the ship was fit to get them where they were directed, and these preparations for war came as a bit of a shock. He also had some friends on the ships that were sunk in the main battle area. It was not a good experience.

Back at home, Liz struggled to finish her dissertation, her school work and to include visits to her mother at weekends. Her father had been told that he must never have a drink again, but he was feeling better. Her mother had been a good nurse but was worn out with the effort she had made at her age. She was badly in need of a holiday.

'I never thought I should get to the end of this term. I've just about finished my dissertation. Haven't seen much of the tutor though. There has been too much going on for that. We have been up with Mum most weekends, but Dad is better. No more drinking for him! Mum is pretty well worn out. She has done really well for her age Thank goodness the war is over and the task force is returning. Will expects to be back mid-August. This time, we really will be able to meet the ship!'

First of all, Liz's dad said that her mother needed a holiday, and he would look after the girls and dogs while Liz and her mum were away. She needed a bit of TLC, and he had booked a hotel for them. He said she had been absolutely marvellous and he wouldn't have pulled through without her. It was good to hear him so appreciative. He had rather taken her for granted for many years and was intolerant of her hearing problems. Giving up drinking had obviously done him good.

Liz thought that a holiday with her mum would do her good as well.

It was the holiday from hell!

Her mother treated it like therapy and spelled out all the unhappiness she suffered throughout her marriage. It was amazing that they were still together. They had not had the option of going their separate ways in their day, and she had given up work when she married so was never independent.

Liz's dad had had a couple of affairs, and her mum's life had been poisoned by them. Liz would never have to stick what she had suffered, as she had always made sure that she could be independent and she resolved never to suffer the humiliation that her mother had endured because of her father's attitude when he had been out drinking. At least, after the hepatitis he would never be able to drink again.

At the end of the week, Liz's mother felt much better and ready to get on with her life. Liz had given up smoking. If ever she had needed a cigarette, it was then and she couldn't even get away to light up!

The girls were so, so glad to see her back. Apparently, they had been bossed about by their grandfather until they and their friends had taken refuge in Kermit's, out of the way of the smell of him cooking tripe, which is what he had decided was the best diet for his recovery. Liz was pleased that they had a good week too!

They, all three, had new suits and hats as they went to Chatham to meet the ship. Some of the crew had been sent home early so that when the ship docked, they would be back on board and Will too would be able to go on leave. Jane was so pleased to go and see her hero daddy, and everyone was much relieved that they were all coming safely back after all that time and danger.

All the families were peering for the first sight of the ship with her signing off pennant, accompanied by the tugs with fire hoses shooting up fountains of water and hooting in welcome. Everyone started waving and cheering and soon dignity was thrown to the winds and hats sailed into the air as loved ones were spotted. Liz doubted that Will would see his grown up young ladies climbing up the railings as usually he was in the engine room at that stage. The ship came closer and, suddenly, a familiar face appeared behind the others. Off came Liz's hat too as she shouted to the girls, "It's Daddy over there!" Then the families went on board and there were hugs all round. They went down to Will's cabin and saw how he had been surrounded by photos of his girls and his dogs all this time. Better still, he was able to come on leave straight away, so they all went back home together.

They stopped for a pub meal on the way, and there was a lot to say and tell as the girls brought him up to date with their doings, chattering nineteen to the dozen and looking at him as if they still couldn't believe their eyes. He didn't have a chance to say much.

The dogs were delirious with joy, as their master appeared and took them for a short run down the road to uncross their legs.

Then, he was off down to the pub. Liz felt very flat after all the excitement and the long drives, and her hopes that things might somehow be different now that he knew how important he was to them all and how much they had longed for his safe return. The girls went down the road to tell their friends, and Liz and the dogs just looked at each other.

Chapter Fifteen
Aftermath

Will had some leave, did some gardening and took up his pub timetable again. I went back to school. Ann to college, Jane to boarding school, Will got another posting to the engineering school in Gosport. Mixture as before.

We never did hear what went on in the war, but I got the idea that there were some nasty patches. He woke up last night in the middle of a nightmare. He couldn't say what, but he was shaking for ages. That on top of the drinking and snoring it doesn't make for a good bedtime experience. I just wish he would talk to me. It can't be good to bottle everything up.

He is not a pleasant person to be near when he has been drinking like that. We are always in the wrong. He didn't even make a favourable comment on the new extension, even though the paint was still tacky on the front door when he got home. He has no idea of what we had to put up with or that we worried ourselves silly about him while the war was going on. It is as if he is trying to shut everything out or drown it all. He always seems to have a drink in his hand from the moment he comes home and probably one or two at lunch time too. One of his old friends was on HMS Sheffield. I wonder how he is taking it.

Jane was quite pleased to go back to school. Her hero has developed leaden feet. The girls complain that they cannot do anything right and they are not sailors with orders to obey. They had enough when their grandfather was in charge, but at least it was only temporary. Only the dogs are happy. They are very forgiving and sit at his feet like twin statues.

We don't get the college kids calling in any more.

Chapter Sixteen
Time for Changes – Liz

Despite my degree and everything, I was advised that I was too old for promotion. If they think that I am going to continue on the bottom rung until I retire, they will have to think again. I am worth more than that.

I will give it another term. Jane does her O-levels in a couple of weeks' time and after that she says that she too is coming home to sixth form college. It is a pity, for she would have been a prefect next year, but I can understand her wanting to come home and Ann will be glad to have her around. So shall I. I can't say how much I have missed them these years, but I felt that it was for the best to give them a good start in life. Since they had the opportunity of private education they were better out of the state system in these times of strange ideas. The school where I am has more of the old values of hard work and discipline, and even my German teacher friend came to join us there, but there is such a variation in quality of education even just in this area. I am pleased that I have fulfilled my long held ambition to be a French teacher and I have had an O-level class this year. I hope they do well.

Jane is going to join Ann working in the pub on Sundays so that will be two lots of stinking clothes to wash! Ann was 18 a few days ago, but Jane will be only 15 when she leaves school, so not going on to college is not an option. They will go to different ones anyway as Ann wants to do an extra year. I wonder why?

I've booked a proper holiday for us this year and there will be no excuses from Will as he has a set leave time at the engineering school. He is enjoying this job as he is the head of the section that deals with new recruits after their initial training at Plymouth. He gets on well with his staff and the lads,

I just wish that he could make the same bond with females! At least with his own females!

We are going to Greece to stay in a hotel. No more caravan holidays, dogs or cold seas! It will be such a change!

Talk about a guard-dad! He just hasn't been able to relax at all. It is just because Ann had an attendant waiter pandering to her newly acquired vegetarian tastes and inviting her out. He is nothing like as bad as some of the boyfriends I have seen her out with, but then, it is the first time that Will has really had anything to do with teenage girls. His hackles were up and he was practically growling! He will just have to get used to the idea that his little girls are nearly grown-up. He has missed so much these past few years.

It is the first package holiday we have been on and I have really enjoyed it. I even got him up to dance at the disco and it was quite like old times. Embarrassing for the girls though!

It is much more fun when he is away from the pub routine. A bottle of wine with our dinner, now that is much more civilised. I could get used to this!

Well, we are all settled for the next school year. Jane is doing science A-levels, as she has decided she wants to be a chiropractor. She passed all her O-levels well except one and was most upset when I asked why.

Ann passed her A-level English, to spite her teacher again I guess, but to my amazement failed her biology that was her favourite subject. Maths went down the drain again, now she has decided to do a course as a dental surgery assistant. I told her that that was way below her capabilities, but she is set on it. We shall see how it turns out. I think her confidence has taken a knock again, or maybe a simple course will leave more time for socialising.

At least now that we don't have to pay for boarding school, my salary is not so important, and I can look to see what there is outside teaching. I'm fed up with the appalling behaviour of some of the pupils. I'm not going to stick at this for another 15 years. It is time to look for a fresh start, preferably with good financial prospects. I am getting worried about Will's drinking habits.

That's it. I have resigned. I have found a job that I am not too old for. My colleagues think I am brave to have given up teaching, but I can't face stress at work as well as at home. Something has to give. I'm not ready to give up on my marriage for the sake of the girls, but the atmosphere is certainly not pleasant. Will's drinking has got worse. He can scarcely wait for the pubs to open and when he gets back he drinks lager until he can barely stagger upstairs. Then, the snoring makes the house ring. The girls turn up their music, a different record from each bedroom. I can't even go out and, anyway, where could I go? There are always books to be marked.

My new job is in Life Assurance, and it will be quite a change. I've done a few trial visits and when I start in the New Year, there will be a number of residential courses to go on and a fair bit of work in the evenings with time off during the day. I can't wait!

It is so embarrassing! My new boss wanted to meet my husband and when he called, there he was, drunk in his armchair. He woke up and burbled, very unsteady on his feet. That is the last time I bring anybody home. No wonder we never see anything of the girls' friends now.

He might as well be still away for all the company I get. I even take the dogs out for somebody to talk to. I quite enjoy going out for a walk during the day and then getting down to things at night. I'm feeling better about myself since I left teaching. It is nice to get dressed up for work instead of wearing something that is proof against splinters, ink and chewing gum. I enjoy going out to meet people and cold calling, even on the telephone. Most people are pleasant and polite, not like at school, and you can always go away if they are not. It is good to have an adult to talk to, and it didn't take long to have all the information at my fingertips.

The incubus in the corner has made me more depressed than I realised. Gloom is catching and there is a real black cloud emanating from him. It was dragging me down as well. The girls say I am much more relaxed since I left teaching and I feel it, most of the time…until I get home again.

I really had to lay it on the line for Will when he came home tonight.

Jane came home from college most upset. She wouldn't tell me what the matter was, so of course I worried. Finally, Ann told me what the trouble was. One of Jane's friends had been describing this man he had seen in a pub. He was so drunk that he kept falling off the bar stool. Everyone was laughing until it became clear that the pathetic drunk at the pub where they worked was Will. Someone turned round to Jane and asked, "Isn't that your dad?" She ran off in tears.

By the time I had finished the story, Will was in tears as well. He made a solemn promise never to go down that pub again, ever, even though it had been his local for many years, ever since we moved house. He doesn't want his daughters hurt.

Well, he is keeping his promise, but that means doing all his drinking at home. Probably that has cut it down a bit as he has made an effort to be more pleasant lately. The only trouble is that suddenly his mood will change and he accuses me of keeping him away from his friends. Friends! There is nobody who cares about him a bit or they would never have let him get in such a state. If I ever say anything, I am nagging and sometimes in his drunken dreams he calls me all sorts of names.

The girls are getting on alright with their college courses now, and I have just done a course about pensions. It is quite frightening how much you should have in a pension pot to have a hope of retirement. I went into my old office today and met some of those I used to work with all those years ago. I didn't do any business, but I did find out that I could have returned to the Civil Service instead of starting teaching, apparently the rules changed I shall have to bear that in mind if I find I need a more stable job.

Will and I went for a day out together and did some straight talking. He is going to try to cut down on his drinking, as I believe it is beginning to show at work. After an evening on the booze it must be difficult to be all bright and shiny in the morning, even though it is an old Navy tradition. He says he can take it or leave it. I hope he is right. He is good company when he is sober and I enjoyed our day out.

Ann has finished her course as a dental nurse and has got a job a few miles away. She has bought a scooter to get to work. Scary! She has to get to work somehow and the buses do not run right, but for a girl with no sense of direction and not a lot of road sense, it is frightening. I worry wherever she is and Will says I should cut the umbilical cord someday. But then, I've only told him the half of it.

So family holidays are out this year. Sighs of relief all round, and Jane says she doesn't mind a bit.

Will and I are going to John O'Groats by train. That will be a change. Will says he won't drink on holiday. He says he doesn't need it and can do without it, so that will be a change too!

We had a good holiday with spectacular scenery. We even hired a car and drove all over the top, over mountains and alongside lochs and the north coast. Will kept his word except when we visited a distillery. You couldn't expect him to give up a tasting. I hope he keeps off the drink when we get home.

We don't see much of the girls these days. They both have boyfriends in the same crowd, but needless to say, they don't bring them home. Will is back to the lager and the stump.

He looks so lonely there, locked in a world of his own with no room for his family. Even if I go out and speak to him he only grunts. I am the enemy again, standing between him and his drink. When he comes home, he seems alright but by the time he has had a meal and that first drink or two, he seems to withdraw inside himself. It is nearly dark, but he will sit outside on his stump as long as he can and then probably come in and go straight to bed.

I've got to go out and see a client. When I come back, he will be asleep and snoring. It really does not make me want to go near him. I'll sit up reading as long as I can. He doesn't ask me about my work, and I no longer ask about his. The silence is deafening. He still gets those nightmares from time to time, but I can't do anything for him. He usually sleeps more peacefully when I go up but I lie awake for hours. When he is snoring as well, it makes me feel so angry. He is not only robbing me of sleep but of life as well. When did I last go out and enjoy myself?

Jane is engaged and they have set a wedding date for next May. She will only be 19. She finished college when she was only 17, and the chiropractic college said she had to wait for another year. She decided not to go to university despite all my recommendations. Both she and Ann started going out with the boys from the local football team and no longer wanted to leave the area. They said they had already been sent off to boarding school. If only they knew how much I missed them while they were away, but I thought they would get a better education, and I always hoped we would get another shot at a married-accompanied post. Jane wanted to be independent. She took a local job with a bank and is on a management-training course. They obviously recognised her ability.

She and her fiancé are house hunting now, and she will move out when she finds one.

Ann is doing one of the other jobs she applied for. When they asked her at interview why she had chosen the company she admitted she had filled in the form her sister had sent for. Honest to a fault! Ann decided not to join the Navy as a dental hygienist after she was bored silly being a dental surgery assistant. I think she had had enough of sailors after watching her Dad. I suppose she will want to move out after Jane does. Then I shall lose both my daughters again. Ann is now working for BT. It is in customer care and a good thing that the computer does the maths. At least it is a steady job to impress the bank when she too needs a mortgage.

I have changed course again, as I found that selling Life Assurance on commission only demanded a less than totally honest approach to make a good income. I enjoyed meeting people, and it was pleasant not to feel you were on stage all the time trying to keep order, but I am better at teaching and helping folk than selling myself or my own interests. I couldn't give it the single-minded approach I needed for a management role, especially with all the turmoil at home, so I decided to apply for the Civil Service again to work with the employment service which I thought might best use my skills and experience. Now I have to wait until there is a local vacancy, and in the meanwhile, I am going to try supply teaching.

I did enjoy the freedom for a few years, but in the long term, I have chosen security. The pension business is enough to make you very aware of this.

Will has noticed that I have changed my job, so he must be improving. I am supply teaching at all my old schools. They think more of supply teachers than they used to of the regular staff so it is nice to be back, but even nicer to know that it is only temporary. Supply teaching is a challenge. You never know how much will be left for you or whether you will have to play it by ear. You never know your timetable until you get there, but that suits me. I have taught such a range of subjects that there is usually no problem and the schools have a wider range of textbooks now, not many worksheets at all! It still makes me realise that I was right to leave when I did. My colleagues look even more stressed than I did! Nice to move on.

Oh how the Civil Service has changed! I remember the days of "I am, sir, your obedient servant, sir". Now it is all casual and Christian names. It is really difficult to work out who is the boss and the dress code has gone out of the window. Even the big white chief is walking around in shirt-sleeves! I think it works better though once you get the hang of it. It is a bit of a culture shock at present. When talking on the phone, you have to be very wary. Chris could be male or female, your boss or your colleague or even a member of the public. You have to recognise the voice or play the game of 'Give us a clue'.

I didn't get much benefit from all those years I spent in the service before. It was back to the same grade as when I left school as my temporary promotion for the Census did not make much difference. Even the pay scale is not far off the basic, as they have only about seven steps instead of the 35 when I started work. At least, I have a few years on my pension because I was too late to reclaim it when we got married. Lucky really.

I am involved in the Restart programme to get people back into work after they have been unemployed for many years. A lot have suffered ill health, some are just bewildered about how to start looking for work especially if they have had little experience of working or have only been in one job before, and a lot have been let down by the education system. I met some pretty difficult kids when I was teaching, but you can't help feeling sorry for those who are functionally illiterate but would really like to work. I've seen some nice young men in their mid-twenties who messed about at school (I can believe that) and now have several children of their own and labouring jobs have disappeared, so they will never make enough money to keep their family unless they go back to education and fill in the gaps and learn a new skill. It is a long hard route. I don't think many will stick it. How often have I heard the words "If only I knew then what I know now." I heartily agree, but talking to them at school had no effect.

My background in education should enable me to bring something extra to this job. First, I have lots of courses to go on, and I love going on courses!

I'm really enjoying this job, but promotion is not on the horizon. I'm back where I was at 18. It is still dead men's shoes unless you are lucky. Still, it isn't as stressful as teaching and more reliable than commission only! I shall just have to bide my time and keep an eye open for opportunities. At least, I think I am doing something worthwhile. It is quite amazing to see the impact that technology has had on jobs. You really need some computer skills now even to work in a warehouse. The other thing is where there used to be a driver and a mate in a lorry, the mate is redundant and he is the one with reading problems. One that really stuck in my mind was a driver who couldn't read and recognised road signs by the general shape. I'm glad I never followed him on a road!

I met an old friend from the early days in London. He is divorced and living about 20 miles away, not far from where I am working now. I've bent his ear a few times when things got on top of me. He advised me to pack it in and get a life, but I'm not ready to give up on my marriage yet.

I do get fed up when I get home from work and find that Will is already home and drunk. I've turned round several times and gone over to my friend's house for the evening. The girls were worried when I arrived back after them...talk about the tables turned!

I don't think my friend is the right man for me, though I might have had an offer if I'd shown any interest. It has just made me realise that I am letting my life go by, all work and no play. I don't think there is any future in my marriage as the sober periods are getting fewer and further apart. It is a very big step to let go though. I suppose there comes a flashpoint when you just know that this is it. It is very wearing. I look at myself in the mirror and don't like the face that stares back. I suppose there is not much to smile about. I just feel I am getting old and life is passing me by.

I got taken out to dinner tonight. That was a surprise. It was nice to get all dressed up.

The moment I got into the car I realised it was a mistake. He was drunk already and certainly not fit to drive. I was terrified as he was all over the road and unaware of just how dangerous it was. We were lucky to get to the restaurant without an accident. I drove back, of course, as I always do. Good thing I rarely drink. Someone has to stay sober in case there is an emergency. It is very worrying, though.

We are going on holiday with Will's brother and his wife. Perhaps, that will shake him up a bit. They were thinking about going on holiday to France on a boat on the Canal du Midi. It has been years since we had that canal boat holiday when the girls were small. Danny has always been keen on canals, and I don't mind driving and acting as interpreter. We will spend a week in the car and a week on the boat. I am looking forward to it and have already found a book of routes through France.

It took three days for him to sober up and realise where we were. So much for my navigator! He didn't have a clue what was going on and Danny was quite shocked to see him so bad. There is hard drinking – they are all used to that – but to be totally disconnected from the rest of the world, that is way beyond just drinking too much. He was alright when he came to, and we had a pretty good holiday after that and a lot of laughs. It was a lot of driving but that was OK by me, and at least, I am used to driving in France.

Long dark evenings again. It doesn't help anything. Jane is getting married in May, but they have found a house and she will be moving out of here shortly. I can't see Ann staying at home any longer than she has to, but her boyfriend has no idea of saving and neither has she, but at least we saved for her as a child so she will have enough for a deposit. I can't say I am looking forward to Christmas this year. I don't feel much like celebrating. Work is going alright, but very busy.

The house is very dark now that one of our chicks has flown and the other is rarely there. I wonder why we bothered with that extension. I'm considering moving into the spare bedroom to get away from the snoring. There doesn't seem much reason for sharing a bed.

I look on him with disgust sometimes. It is sheer greed to keep on drinking until you are unconscious. How on earth he gets by at work, I shall never know. At least, his job is mainly paper based now. He seems to get home early quite often saying that his lads have told him they can manage without him. I bet!

I didn't think it would last long. Ann has found a house that they can afford and she is going to move out too. It is a former council house and will need decorating but at least that makes it cheaper. They might as well get on the housing ladder as prices are going up all the time. I expect that I can find plenty of things to start her off, as she will not have much in the kitty once the deposit and fees have been paid. I shall miss her.

Preparations are going ahead for Jane's wedding. She has been writing lists for ages and seems to have everything under control. I have managed to get my friend to cater for her. What is good enough for Henley Regatta should be good enough for us. Now, all we want is good weather. I hope Will doesn't disgrace us. I have asked Danny to keep an eye on him. By the time it is all over, my nerves will be shot to shreds! I have booked a holiday in the sun for myself when it is all over. Things will seem flat after all the excitement. I want to see how I can get on by myself on holiday. It has been a long winter.

The wedding went well and a very proud father wore his uniform to give her away and his sword was used to cut the cake. We had a lovely day and managed to keep things peaceful. Everyone enjoyed it from the relatives to the youngsters who came for the evening BBQ. I'm looking forward to my holiday now.

It really is strange to be on my own with nobody else to consider. First time ever on holiday. I get up when I feel like it, wander down to breakfast in the taverna – coffee and Greek yoghurt and honey, yummy – then it is off to the beach for a bake in the sun until the sea calls. It is the first time that I have been to a Greek island. I can't get over the clarity of the water and it is warm too. It beats freezing in Dorset. I'm glad I brought several books to read. It helps when you are on your own, especially waiting for your meal to arrive. I'm a bit of a people watcher, but I like to have a cover story so it is not too obvious. I may not read too much of the book. Several people have been friendly but it was mainly couples, and I didn't want to impose on them by taking up much of their time. I have been on several excursions through the tour operator and yesterday I walked over to the next beach. The headland didn't look too high from a distance but it certainly tested my new-found fitness. I couldn't have done it when I arrived, but a few days swimming have helped. There has just been a changeover and there is a new arrival, a single man, who is also looking for company. He must be a good 15 years younger than me so there is no romance! It is nice to have someone to talk to.

Home again and I certainly feel better for the break. I have also proved that I can survive on my own, something that you begin to doubt after 20-odd years of marriage.

Home hasn't changed much. He is even more morose, if anything. It is not as if it is the first time that I have been away, look at all those residential courses. It is almost as if he can hear the thoughts that are beginning to cross my mind. I am going to have to talk to someone about the possibility of a divorce. I really don't know how you go about it.

The sulking has got worse. I mean it is not as if we have always been in each other's pockets. I suppose it was because I didn't discuss my plans before I went. Also, I suppose it is the first time I have gone off entirely on my own. I might not have had anyone to talk to on holiday, but honestly I haven't here either. Thank goodness for work.

Ann has just announced that she is pregnant, and they would like to get married in August. That is going to cause a bit of planning, for with the best will in the world, she hasn't got it under control like Jane had. It may be a register office wedding but it is not going to be a second rate one like we had. We have plenty of room here and have catered for big parties before, so we can have the reception at home with as many of the trimmings as I can make. It will give me something to think about and might even get Will motivated, as, despite everything, he thinks the world of his daughters.

It was a good day, even for a DIY wedding – from the dress, the flowers, the reception at home (thank goodness for a lovely sunny day) to catering for the evening party. Will was on his best behaviour, and we really worked together to make it a successful day. I'm glad that we have no more daughters, as it has been non-stop since the day she said they were getting married and couldn't find a dress to fit her.

With a great effort of will, Will is able to stop drinking for several weeks at a time, but then the depression takes over and he reaches for the usual cure, the bottle. He is troubled by dreams too and I hear him rambling on in his bedroom at night. I feel really sorry for him, but I have given him the ultimatum several times. "It is either me or the bottle." He seems to have chosen the bottle.

If it had been another woman, I might have been able to fight, but alcohol is so insidious. I can't fight the bottle. God knows, I try hard enough, when he is sober enough to talk to. "I still love you!" he professes in tears. Not as much as he loves the bottle, I'm afraid.

I don't believe him anymore. Surely, if he really meant it he would seek medical help. In my job I've met alcoholics who had been worse than he is, but they couldn't escape without help. It is the wretched Naval training. Cover up! Don't admit you need help! Never mind that it is making me ill as well. I keep bursting into tears even at work. How can you counsel anyone when you are a heap yourself? Thank goodness for doughnut-days!

This evening when I got in, I stood at the bottom of the stairs and heard him vilifying me because I got between him and his drinking. Who was he talking to? His dead mother. I had never heard him calling anyone such bad names, let alone me. They say you never overhear anything good about yourself. He seemed furious because I empty away any booze bottles and tell him they do more good down the drain than inside him. I went upstairs and found him fast asleep. It was in his dreams that I had become an ogre. The man I used to love has become a shambling incoherent heap. I have lost all respect for him. You need trust and respect in a marriage.

Despite the few hectic days of making Ann's wedding work, we are back to the same situation, and I have taken legal advice about a divorce. I simply cannot hold my own life together with all the stress. I burst into tears again today at work for no particular reason. I have got to be able to hold down my own job. The alcoholics I have met have all said that you have to really reach rock bottom to realise that you have to do something about recovery. I know it is not easy, in fact, very hard to admit you need help and it is well-nigh impossible to recover without intervention and you have to have the will to change things. Perhaps, the threat of a divorce will make Will sit up and consider where his priorities are. One thing is certain. We can't go on like this. I certainly can't. It is wearing me down and I have to protect my own health and sanity.

I'm writing things down as the lawyer advised. It makes pretty depressing reading.

I'm looking forward to the course next week. 'Stress Management'. Whose stress? I wonder.

Chapter Seventeen
Divided

The course was a revelation. The people leading the course were pretty perceptive and the tricks of the trade were very skilful. The students had to draw a picture to describe themselves and their lives. Liz drew a picture of a figure in a tangle of barbed wire. She hadn't realised that she felt as bad as that. Now, she would have to find the way to unravel it.

Most of the other students had a pretty stressful situation in their lives. It seemed that stress management courses were fairly self-selecting. First, you had to identify your own problems before you could begin to help others.

Another exercise showed Liz that she wanted to be recognised as still a relatively young woman, not an old has-been and it was time to take herself in hand again. Being in that kind of a stressful situation was but a small step to losing your own self-belief, and it was important to be kind to yourself as well as to others. Until you really know yourself you cannot help others effectively. It was like being back on the counselling course again.

Liz got in touch with the lawyer to get things moving.

'I have given him one more chance with a holiday in Scotland again, to use up the last of his rail warrants. I hope that getting away from his normal routine will help him to think about things. We are taking the sleeper to Perth and will drive around from there. If he can stay sober, we might have a chance. If not, the papers will be served.

'Scotland was a real struggle. He was drunk when we set off, and I had to drive and navigate through London to pick up the train. At least, I was in my own car.

'By the time we reached Perth, he was better but had a real struggle not to go for a drink. He failed. Although he didn't drink much, it was obvious that he couldn't do without it by force of will as previously and it was a fairly miserable time for both of us. The papers will be served. What a sad end to a marriage that we put everything into.'

Liz authorised that the divorce papers should be served on their return.

Just a few weeks later, Will was informed that his Naval career would end without further renewal. He announced that with retirement he had absolutely no intention of working ever again. He was 53. Liz couldn't bear to think of the prospect of him sitting all day and just rotting away, going downhill faster than ever. She begged him to seek medical help, but that would lose face. Whatever face did he think he still had when he was regularly drunk and out of his tree?

Liz applied for a job back nearer her parents so that she could stay with them until the family home was sold. She just had to wait things out in the meanwhile. The house was large enough for them to be able to lead separate lives, and the current market value would enable them both to buy a smaller property when it was sold.

In retirement, Will fulfilled all Liz's worst predictions. He spent all day drinking and sulking. He didn't even pretend to take an interest in the garden and not much in the dogs. Liz was quite glad that it was no longer her problem. She didn't get the job she was after, but was still on the shortlist for promotion when another job came up. She was busy at work and didn't try to get home early.

Will didn't argue with the conditions of the divorce, except that he said that he didn't realise that he had been so awful. Liz thought that the worst thing was that he still didn't realise just how bad he was. She showed him the notes she had made. Will cried and went out with a bottle.

He was still reluctant to accept medical help, and Liz was glad that he didn't attempt to drive himself to a pub and cause an accident.

The lawyer had said that although they could share the same house, Liz wasn't to do anything for Will and they should lead completely separate lives. At the top of the market the value of the house was enough for them both to get a smaller dwelling and Liz hoped they would find a buyer before long and before it fell into disrepair as Will took no interest in either house or garden. He got more and more morose and didn't seem to be interested in anything. Liz was still worried about him and his state of mind and couldn't persuade him to go to a doctor even though he was now out of the Navy.

Liz's uncle died and since he hadn't left a will his house went to his two sisters. This gave Liz a potential toehold in her home town. If she could buy out her aunt, her mother would give her the other half of the house. She could go home! Where they were living was no longer home to her, despite having her daughters nearby in their homes. The house she shared with Will was now a hollow shell, with far more bad memories than good. Even if she could not get an immediate transfer, she could get the old cottage habitable (it would need a lot of work on it) and put in for a sideways move. She could go up at weekends and work on the house, rather than inflict herself on her daughters. There was plenty of time for that when the baby came, and she would be transformed into a doting grandmother.

"I didn't really mean that about a doting granny, but I am!" said Liz happily. "She is so lovely. We are all so proud of her, and Ann makes a lovely mum." Robyn was born in the same hospital as her mum had been and Liz was reminded of all the high hopes they had had when Ann made her appearance. She could scarcely believe that the little family had fallen apart despite all their good intentions at the beginning. *I do hope that Ann will not have the same kind of problems*, thought Liz, worriedly.

'I have managed to get a mortgage to buy my aunt out of my uncle's house. Now, I can begin to make it mine even though there is no sign of a job up here yet. It makes a good bolt hole and gives me a chance to get away and work in my own garden rather than grieve over what ought to have been done down here. I have to keep Dad at bay, though, otherwise he would plant my garden with cabbages instead of flowers and things I want. It was good of Will to commute some of his pension to pay off the mortgage or I would not have been able to have one here. I can't afford to pay for the garden as well as the house, but I shall be good for that later when we have sold. Good thing it is in the family.'

There was so much to be done to the house, although, her uncle had built an extension at the rear to make a kitchen and bathroom, Liz was not going to keep that arrangement. The front room was right on the main road with lots of traffic noise so that would become the kitchen, as Liz had no intention of spending much time cooking. That had been done enough when there was a family. With just one person it wouldn't take up much time at all. The new kitchen floor was concrete, once the old flagstones had been replaced, and Liz took on the task of covering it with ceramic tiles. The fact that she had never done any tiling before did not deter her, that it was mid-winter and there was no heat could be coped with, but when her mother kept offering to help, life got very difficult. The end result was not perfect but it was better than having clouds of concrete dust every time you moved.

Liz's approach to DIY bore no resemblance to Will's perfectionism, she just got it done.

In the sales, she was able to purchase units for the kitchen and the builder was very tolerant and worked round her to make the place habitable during the short winter days. The main house had had nothing done to it for decades and when the wallpaper came off so did a lot of the plaster. The bedroom above the kitchen was transformed into a bathroom and, for the rest, Liz was busy with tins and tins of emulsion paint. Luckily, the ceilings were low, so there was no ladder work. Liz came up at weekends, and after freezing in the new house, was very pleased to get back to her parents to sleep and get warm again.

It pained her to think of the big house in the south, being left to rot, as the housing market had slumped since she had bought out her aunt. She needed it to sell so that she could build on an extension to give the little house more room and make up for the bedroom that had been made into a bathroom. The builder did what he could on the tight budget, but the rest would have to wait. When the sun came out and the days turned warmer, Liz was able to get out into the garden and have a dig. That got rid of a lot of frustration that built up during the week. It was very hard sharing a house with someone you had divorced, and the lawyer advised her that they had to keep completely separate lives until the decree absolute was finalised. Even though they shared a kitchen, she was not to share any meals or do his washing or anything. All she could do was watch the man deteriorate even further, as well as the house.

He still didn't seem to realise why it was that she had been driven to divorce him, and it had given him no incentive to change. In fact, if anything, he was drinking more and the garden was such a wreck that Liz had to sacrifice one of her weekends away to trying to bring some semblance of order to the garden at the big house. The whole place was getting less and less saleable, as there had been no maintenance to either house or garden. He seemed to spend all his time slumped in his chair and drinking and that was all. It was exactly what he had said when he left the Navy. How could he do nothing all day? He had a major case of depression but still refused to get medical help. "You don't understand," he muttered. She did, all too well, after talking to her alcoholic clients at work, but unless he took matters into his own hands, nobody could help him. It grieved her to see the man she had married fall into such a state.

'I have got a transfer! Promotion seems to be on permanent hold but, at least, I can transfer in the same grade (the same as when I left school), and there is always a hope of better things. It is a whole new set-up that the Government has made with a combination of staff with employment service background and others who have been in various businesses. I have experience of both so it should be helpful. At least, I shall be able to go back home and live in my own place, and I shall just have to go back south to visit the girls. There is a lot to be done before it is habitable.

'The builder has pulled out all the stops and even put a door on the bathroom when my friend came to visit at Easter. Her son was in hospital in Bristol, and she helped me with the last of the painting in the mornings before we went to visit him in the afternoons. He had tried to commit suicide. He had his first epileptic fit on his 18th birthday and he has got worse and worse. It is a really nasty illness, particularly for a young lad on the brink of manhood. He never got to drive his birthday car. His mum has been torturing herself that it might somehow be her fault as she has just divorced her husband who announced on their 25th anniversary that he had found a new girlfriend. "Men!" she said. She was really upset until she thought what

133

good men were for…bringing in the coal. "And then I realised we had central heating!"

'I have got to wait until our house is sold before I can build a new extension to make up for the lost bedroom, unless of course I can get a further loan. The garden looks quite good even if it is planted up with veggies. But I have got a lawn. That worked off an awful lot of frustration. The shrubs have taken too. And I've got strawberries and raspberries. It is beginning to look like home.

'I start my new job tomorrow. I'm excited. It will be good to travel to work through country lanes instead of being stuck in traffic on the motorway. I can sleep at Mum and Dad's until everything is ready.'

***

Liz started her new job and made friends with her new colleagues. Even having to crawl behind herds of cows in the mornings was better than the struggle on the motorway in the south and coming home in the evenings through the country lanes made her sing even before she reached her new home.

Will had finally realised that she had gone for good. He was still ever so depressed but had actually been to see a doctor, so that was a breakthrough.

He offered to take Liz away on holiday to the Seychelles and Mauritius and even promised not to drink if she would go. It was an offer she couldn't refuse as there was no prospect of any other holiday. What a pity he had left it so late. He booked up the holiday and even tried to control his drinking. They got on much better once she had finally left and when she went down to see the girls, it was alright staying with Will.

Ann's baby was growing into a fine little girl, a real personality in her own right, and she enjoyed running round the lawn which was better kept now. Ann looked dreadfully tired, she was waitressing and washing up evenings as she had to earn some money to keep them. Her husband was a wastrel, a good workman but a heavy drinker, leaving no money for the family At least, Will always put the family first and didn't drink when the girls were small.

The holiday in the Seychelles and Mauritius was a great success and Will managed to stay on the wagon, so they both came back refreshed and happy. He was always a different person away from his home rut, and they really enjoyed each other's company. If only it would last.

Work was going well in Liz's new post. She soon had her finger on all the buttons but had to tread carefully for fear of upsetting her superiors. So what was new? She had had lots of practise at that, treading carefully in all aspects of her life. It didn't mean that she liked it any more. It was the usual problem of incompetent chiefs and Indians with all the experience. Such was the invention of the quango. At least, it was in the location where she wanted to be.

It was a good thing that the job was busy because there was no movement on selling the house, and it was beginning to be in need of a really good clean. Buyers and even lookers had dried up and Will was reluctant to drop the price in line with the fall in the market. He was drinking again though not so badly as before. He was probably bored doing nothing all day, and he didn't have any hobbies or even friends to visit. Even the dogs no longer got long walks as they were beginning to get too old to want to go far anyway.

***

That Christmas, Liz faced a dilemma. She had never left Will alone for Christmas if he was in the country even though it sometimes ended in tears and she was torn between being with her parents, who were getting really old, and spending time with Will. The girls had agreed to spend Christmas together so that was good. As usual, Liz went for a compromise. She brought down the presents for the girls, made the preparations for the Christmas lunch and then shot off back to see the old people, to stay overnight and return to find that Will had cooked the bird as he always did and then get on with their Christmas dinner. The girls would come for Boxing Day lunch which was everyone's favourite. That was the theory.

When she returned Christmas morning, after a foggy and frosty drive, she was looking forward to a warm kitchen smelling of cooking dinner with just the finishing touches to do.

So where was it? The house was cold and Will was in bed, really groggy after heavy drinking the day before. He had forgotten that she was coming back, wondered what all the food was doing and put it all away in the freezer.

So much for Christmas lunch. It had to be thawed out for the following day and the girls would just have to have a hot meal instead of the leftovers they were looking forward to eating. Liz had an omelette and went down to the beach to have a really good cry and get it all over before daring to speak to anyone. So that was another Christmas ruined for her. The girls were alright and the whole episode had passed Will by. He was on a different planet.

Ann announced that she was pregnant again, so that was an end to her getting any sort of better paid job. No wonder she was looking so tired. Liz just hoped that her husband would begin to offer her a bit of support in the home as well as financially. She didn't hold her breath though.

Why are men such parasites, surely they can't all be the same? she thought. Ann would need all the support she could offer.

The baby came in the summer and was another girl. She looked so much like Jane that Liz was sure that she would get the names mixed up. Liz took her leave to help Ann when she came out of hospital and also to look after Robyn who was so proud of her little sister. There was the same gap between Ann's girls as between Ann and Jane. Liz hoped that they would also grow up good friends. It was lucky she could stay with Will when she came down. The house meant nothing to her now as it was full of bad memories, but it was convenient for this time when her daughter needed her. Her own home was a much happier place, and the building work had started again, but slowly.

Jane had a miscarriage, but it must have been doubly hard for her when her sister now had two lovely daughters. She left her husband and went back to her father. That must have been real desperation. Apparently, her husband didn't recognise how bad she felt after the miscarriage, and she was so depressed that her doctor put her on pills. As a result, she got two speeding fines in no time at all. After this, she went back to her husband

and he was so concerned that he was treating her like a princess for a while. At least, he got the message.

Disaster struck again! Liz slipped as she was coming downstairs at home and broke her leg again. It was a spindle staircase and the stair mat was covering a place where the wood had been eaten away and Liz fell down the last two steps. As she looked at her leg, she recognised the sign of a spectacular break again. At least, she was on the ground floor and able to crawl to the phone so that her dad could come and let the ambulance men in. She was supposed to be looking after the old folk, not having to turn to them for help! At least, with his medical background, her father didn't turn a hair and soon had her organised and ready to go.

At the hospital, the doctor decided to treat the fracture conservatively. All very well for them. Liz looked at her plaster, stretching from thigh to toes. There was no way that she could stay in her own home or even her parents' as the bathrooms were upstairs. There was nothing else for it, she would have to go and live with Will. There was plenty of room in the big house and she could have a bed downstairs near the cloakroom loo. Until the builder got on with her extension and the downstairs loo or Liz got a walking plaster, she would just have to rely on other people for some months. At least, it would give Will something to do.

Liz was stuck in a wheelchair with her leg extended in front of her, helpless and angry at getting into such a position, though, there was no indication that the stairs were defective. It was just bad luck. She had wanted to see more of the family but hadn't expected it to be this way. You had to feel positive about some aspect.

Will was happy to come up and fetch her from the hospital, to arrange the ground floor so that she could get around on crutches (how much weight had she put on since the last time!) and even took her out every day for a walk in her wheelchair. He soon developed good arm muscles. Liz knew it was a heavy weight, for she felt it when she moved around on crutches. A full-length plaster was heavy in itself.

When they went back a month later to see how the fracture was progressing, they planned to see the builder and also her parents. The doctor said that the fracture wasn't healing and she would have to stay in plaster much longer than was usual. When she asked why they hadn't pinned the fracture, she was told that this treatment was good experience for the trainee orthopaedic doctor. They hadn't considered its effect on her career or her blood pressure! It was just lucky that Will was prepared to look after her, that the house hadn't been sold and that she had more opportunity to see the girls growing up. She tried to focus on the positives.

Ann's new baby was growing well and both of them enjoyed the big garden to play in. At that age, a level lawn was better than one on a hillside like Liz's new garden. The weather was good and Will and Liz went down to the beach almost every day, well, not the beach, but the promenade which was wheelchair friendly. Liz wasn't impressed by the invisibility of the person in the chair. Even though, it was blindingly obvious (with a huge white plaster sticking out) what the problem was, people tended to talk over her and ask Will what was the matter. They also found out that many pavements were not really wheelchair friendly. Will's arm muscles were getting stronger, as Liz was definitely putting on weight with all the sitting. She had also been given HRT to help the fracture to heal and that too didn't help her weight.

She should really have been given it 15 years before when she had the early hysterectomy. Perhaps, that might have helped their relationship. Who knows?

It was lucky that Will had bought such a big car when he retired so that he could take her out and to keep hospital appointments. However, Liz was beginning to miss hers, and Will was beginning to take the odd drink again. She felt vulnerable enough without that!

She decided to make an inventory of what to keep and what to save when the house was finally sold. The housing market was beginning to pick up again, and the builder had finished putting in the plumbing in Liz's home. If they gave her a smaller plaster at the next review, she would be able to go home. She would be sorry to leave the girls again but needed to get on with her life.

Will still had no idea of what he would do when the house was finally sold. Liz thought that perhaps he might go up to his hometown where houses were cheap and perhaps he had some old friends, for he only had one of his Navy friends who still kept in touch. He had enjoyed having her to look after but had never seemed to look at any future plans.

With a smaller plaster, Liz was able to go home and to get back to work. One of her colleagues gave her a lift every day and she was soon back into the swing of things and had caught up on office politics. Only her number two was sorry to see her back as she had had six months of holding the reins.

Will came up to take her to her last hospital appointment when the plaster was finally removed after seven months. It was a puny, hairy leg that finally saw daylight and her old ankle injury had become really immobile. She hoped that physiotherapy would help as she didn't want to be crippled with arthritis at her age. The doctor who had recommended conservative treatment told her that if the pain got too much, they would be able to fix the joint permanently as ankle replacements had not been invented. She was not impressed.

Will took her out in her car to see if she was able to drive it. Liz just couldn't depress the clutch so it was impossible. She was so upset.

The next day, he came to meet her from work in a brand new automatic car that she would be able to drive. He had traded in the other and paid the rest as a gift for her. Liz was delighted.

He has been so good to me that I am quite ashamed that I harboured such awful thoughts about him when he started drinking again, I'm glad I didn't say anything then and bit my tongue. It is the drink and not the man. I must focus my anger on the addiction not the person. I just can't bear seeing such a waste of a good man, she thought.

A buyer was at last found for the house once the price had been drastically reduced. It had been on the market for four and a half years and during that time the market dropped and they had to wipe 60,000 pounds off the asking price. All that time nothing had been done to the house, but the market was beginning to rise again and people were looking for potential. It was in a very good location at least. Will needed to make a move before it fell down around his ears. Already there was a nest of field mice indoors. They scampered around the carpet and up the chimney. Will just watched them and the dogs were too old to bother. It was company! The dogs were quite pitiful to see as both suffered from arthritis. They were Will's only companions, and he could not bear to have them put to sleep.

Liz decided to go down to talk to the girls and let them know what to do with the furniture and ornaments which had been left to try to make the house attractive. Will was sunk in lethargy and she was not sure that he would remember what she had said. He was totally incoherent on the phone so was obviously drinking heavily again and he seemed to have had no thought about the future.

She picked a really bad week to go down as Rusty had just died and Copper was on her last legs. Will was a ball of gloom saying that it was the end of his life.

Then Jane was rushed into hospital with a second miscarriage. There was apparently no particular reason for this at a fairly late stage in the pregnancy and she was told that investigations would only be considered after a third. She was perfectly healthy. It was just one of those things. Ann was very supportive of her sister, but Liz felt awful about having to leave them after her weekend. She planned to have some time off to help all round and to have a mega clear up. Nobody else was going to be able to do anything.

When she went back a week or so later, her first job was to take the remaining dog to the vet's. Will just couldn't do it, and Liz cried lots because Copper had been such a friend to her too during the dark days.

'She has always been such a caring animal, looking after her brother all his life and being there for all the members of the family when they needed comfort. She has heard many problems from all of us and seemed to understand and give a paw or a lick when we needed it most. Her soft eyes would offer sympathy and understanding and I'm sure she would have spoken if she could. The other just lolloped around, a puppy all his life, but Copper was a true friend. Will will be devastated.' Liz wept as she held her for the last time, as she was released from pain.

Then, she went back to try to clear up the mess and smell. Both dogs had been incontinent at the end, but Will had just let them be and had sat there in the mess, unseeing and uncaring, sunk in gloom. He had been unwilling to have them put to sleep, for they were his companions too.

It is a far cry from the smart young sailor he used to be when he used to criticise me for my untidiness, thought Liz as she sorted through things and made lists of what to take and what to get rid of. The completion date was not far off and she would need to hire a van to move things up to her home. Since Will had no forward plans, there was a lot she would not have room for as her house had already been occupied for four years. She told the girls to take whatever they wanted.

It was a good thing that she had said that as they were able to prevent their father from throwing out all Liz's most precious things into a skip. *Although I know I shall never get them back again, at least they are still in the family,* she thought.

Will managed to get most of the junk into a skip and the scouts were glad of some things. At completion date, there was still a lot to fit into the self-drive van and because he had no other plans, Will came up with the furniture.

Liz shed no tears over the house as it was full of bad memories. There had been some good times as well when it was Ann's wedding day and the times when the girls were there with her, but on the whole, moving out was a good day and she hoped that Will would be able to start afresh in a new environment. Perhaps, he would be able to think better when he had got over the move.

The girls thought she was mad. "You move away to get away from him and then you let him follow, Mum. You're divorced for goodness sake!"

Chapter Eighteen
Together

We seem to have come to a working arrangement. Will has thrown himself into gardening at my place and is full of projects. It is my house. He is on his best behaviour. I go to work and to see my friends and he talks to all the neighbours. Life in my town is not at all bad. He won't be short of work, for I have a list of projects as long as your arm.

We are going to take Mum and Dad for a short holiday to visit their friends in Cornwall. They will stay with their friends while we have a short tour around. It will be good to have a break as we have been working flat out with the move and everything.

Wow! We are lucky to be alive. The car had a blow out or something just before we got home. We ended up spun around on a motorway roundabout, within feet of crashing down on the carriageway. Perhaps, there was mud on the road or something. Good thing that Will is so strong as he hung on to the wheel and tried to control the skid and stop in time. He must have been pretty tired after driving all that way, though, I did offer to take over a bit earlier. He was just so pleased to be able to do it and to be part of the family again. Fortunately, none of us is badly hurt, though Dad did have his face cut by his glasses and Mum was very shocked. The ambulance men had them checked over at the local hospital.

The car is a write off. I was pleased that neither of us had had a drink that day, though we did have some wine the night before.

Another brand new car has arrived from the same firm as before. They could find no reason for the crash as three of the tyres were ruined by the skid. I'm glad that Mum and Dad have recovered as Will would have been devastated if they had really been injured. He thinks the world of them.

I'm going down to see Ann. She is pregnant again and really wants to move house before the baby comes, as she wants to move to an area with better schools as the local ones are in a really rough catchment area.

I'll offer to help if she can't afford what she needs for now, but only as a loan, as despite all her children, her husband is still not very helpful.

Talk about while the cat's away! Perishing man! I found some bottles in the dustbin so he must have had a real bender while I was down with Ann.

I really like the look of her new house, and it is a good area for the kids. Things are moving swiftly. She certainly gets a move on when she is pregnant, got married the first time, passed her test last time when she could hardly get behind the wheel after hundreds of pounds worth of lessons previously before she gave up, and this time, moving house.

I don't know whether it is blood pressure, but Will has had several episodes where he has nearly passed out. I have had to hang on to him in the garden to prevent him from falling and he has fallen a couple of times when I was not there and had to crawl to the steps to be able to pull himself up on the handrail. I have tried to get him to see the doctor. Fat chance! He shies away from anything medical. He seems to have no warning before it happens.

I hope he hasn't been drinking again, but I can't smell it.

He has been working hard for months all through the summer, but now the weather isn't so good he doesn't have any other hobbies so he doesn't know what to do if he cannot get into the garden. I have suggested evening classes, to go out and meet some more people, but he isn't interested. He only wants to be with me. That doesn't help me at all, as I feel he would be happier with more people to talk to. All the neighbours think he is lovely and he gets on with them all. Just so long, as he is able to keep away from the booze!

Perhaps we need a holiday to look forward to. We shall not see the girls at Christmas, so perhaps then.

Ann has a son! He is a dear little soul with fair curls. I went down for a week when she came out of hospital. Good thing.

Her husband is a pain in the neck and drinking hard. She is going for a sterilisation operation. They can't afford any more children, that's for sure.

Now, for more good news. Jane is pregnant again and all seems to be going well this time. We shall all keep our fingers tightly crossed. I try to get down a couple of times a month to see them all even if it is only for the day. Ann is having a tough time with four children, three little ones and a big one. Her husband is less than no help. At least, Will enjoyed what he saw of our children when he could, and he was always a good provider. When I go down, more often than not, the cupboard is bare, but her husband never runs out of beer. Our first stop is usually the supermarket.

When the cat's away…again! He had been on a binge while I was down with Ann and the house is littered with empties. I was a bit suspicious as he has not been very productive in the garden and was burbling a bit on the phone when I rang.

I am not putting up with it. He can find somewhere else to live. He can come and play in the garden, but I can never be sure that he will do no damage. The rule was no drinking on my premises, so I'll have to tell him. That is why I made it quite clear that it was my home, not ours. He tries to forget sometimes. The neighbours say that he still thinks that we are married, but we are not. He is not my problem anymore, so he can move out. I can't put up with that again.

He has found a bedsit closer to town which is adequate, if not the comforts of home and he has a lovely view over the fields. He seems happy to work in the garden during the day and to potter off when he has finished, perhaps calling in for a drink on the way. He had bought a new television and filled his room with geraniums. It leaves me free to get on with things I have to do.

I have been offered early retirement as the quango wants to lose all the civil servants and just employ its own people. The alternative is to transfer to Bristol or somewhere, and I don't fancy going to work in a city.

They said they wanted to employ staff who have commercial as well as public service experience and although I have that, I am probably too old and know too much to suit them, so I shall take the retirement package and try consultancy work. I shall miss the MBA course that I have been doing through the civil service as I have really enjoyed working with young graduates. It has another year to run but I can't continue if I leave. Just when the Employment Service finally recognised my potential! I've learned enough on this course to put to use as there are a lot of businesses out there that could do with help in management.

Retirement and the Hoover flights promotion! It must be my lucky month. What a good end to my public service career! I have the time and free flights to go to Orlando and visit my cousin. I shall not take Will as he needs to sober himself up again, but I shall travel with another cousin who was good to me while I was in London.

I am sure that there is something wrong with Will besides the booze. Even when I am pretty sure that he has not been drinking he seems to pass out momentarily, and I've had to hold him to stop him falling. I sometimes wonder if it was one of these episodes that caused the crash we had coming back from Cornwall. Perhaps, he ought to have his blood pressure checked again or something. He has had another bout of depression, and I had to have him back here to live for a while to pick up again. He is alright when he is busy in the garden, and spring is coming so there will be lots to do.

Jane has had a baby boy! All is well and I am so relieved. Will and I went down to see her at Easter just for the day, and I shall go back to stay with Ann for a few days to see what I can do for them both.

Will fell down in the garden today and I had to get a neighbour to help to pick him up. He hadn't been drinking as he has been with me for a few days after another bout of depression. I told him that the drink brings on depression, and he promised to stay sober if he could come 'home', but it doesn't last many weeks before he is off again. He doesn't look half as well as he used to. I'm sure there must be something else.

We had Ann and the children up here for a week to give her a bit of a break. They are growing up fast and are really lovely. We all piled into Will's car and took them for days out. It was really good to see them all together. Will enjoyed himself and indulged the kids with lots of ice creams. Any excuse!

We have booked a holiday. There is too much to do in the garden in the summer, and I really must try to get my business off the ground, but it is funny how offers of help vanish when you go to take them up. There is lots of unpaid work and I am trying to finish off two projects I started when I was still in the Service but when it comes to asking for funding it is a different kettle of fish. I shall have done what I set out to do by September and if they don't take it further that is their short-sightedness. At least, I shall feel I have done my best.

I had an almighty row with Ann's husband this weekend. She was really ill after her sterilisation operation, and he helped by leaving his toolbox around so that I found young Harry crawling about with a mouthful of nails. I was not amused. Ann was not amused at the names he called me. Then he made a bonfire of the bed I used to use when I went down there. If he thinks that will stop me visiting, he will be in for a shock.

Chapter Nineteen
Deterioration

I found Will drinking in the greenhouse today. It is hard to tell if he staggers around from drinking or if there is something else wrong with him. I really would like him to get to the doctor but I can't get him to go. In any case, he would probably pull himself together just like for 'Captain's Rounds' and then fall into a heap later.

I threatened him with no holiday after all, but he says he can do it. He is going to stop drinking from now on. He is even going to alcoholics anonymous. The nearest one is about ten miles away, but he says he will do it. I do hope this works. At last, he has admitted he has a problem. That has to be the first step.

Well, he went, twice. He said that everyone was chain-smoking so badly that it nearly choked him. He is not going again, but he is adamant that he can do it himself. We shall see. I'm not holding my breath.

We are off tomorrow. Christmas on the corals! How does that sound? I suggested a mini cruise over the Great Barrier Reef and that is the core. We are taking advantage of stopovers at Fiji and Auckland on the way out and in Tahiti and The Cook Islands on the return leg. We have booked the cruise and the journey from Brisbane to Cairns by train. I am so excited! What a good thing I took retirement so that I can please myself about holidays! All these places I have heard about and have even got the tee-shirts from. Now, I get to see them as well!

The holiday was fantastic and Will kept up the good work all the time. He was so fit and happy and he seemed ten years younger and ready for anything. He particularly enjoyed diving and snorkelling over the reef and was still out with the fish long after everyone else had given up. In fact, one swim was called off because there were jellyfish in the water, but he was away, oblivious to all danger and feasting his eyes on all the brightly coloured fish swimming in and out of the corals. Even I went snorkelling, despite my tendency to drown myself. It was simply magic! At the end of a five-week holiday, we were both relaxed and happy. In fact, it was I who couldn't stand the pace and suffered a tummy-bug when we got to Los Angeles and I introduced him to the fun of Disneyland.

If we can maintain this rapport, it is better than when we were married.

Well, the holiday was great, but when I started work again and there was not much to do in the garden, things began to change. The morning would start off well, but by the afternoon he was different. I haven't found the bottles, but they must be around. It is such a shame as he has a real Jekyll and Hyde personality. I just can't put up with this as he is away with the fairies when he has been drinking and is certainly not to be trusted alone in my house. It is such a shame after he proved he could leave it alone for quite a long time. I really can't be there looking over his shoulder all the time.

He collapsed in the garden again today. There was no way I could help him up, and I had to get my strong neighbour to help me again. He gives them the impression that it is just drinking that does it, but I wish he would go to the doctor. His brain seems to switch off for a few seconds, and if I am not there, he will fall. I suppose that is what happened today.

These falls are becoming more frequent and he has no idea what has happened to him. He is very confused after and smells strange. The last time he had to crawl to the railing by the steps to help himself upon to his feet again. There doesn't seem to be any trigger, one minute he could be talking to you and the next he has fallen. I've asked him if he gets any warning, but he seems to have no reason at all. He doesn't want to go to the doctor in case he gets treatment for depression again. He hates medicines. He would probably have to admit he has been drinking again and he is in denial about that.

I have just been down to Ann for a few days to help out. Against my better judgement I left Will here and he got the DTs. My back windows were covered with red paint as he painted flames to keep the wolves away and he smashed down a clump of lupins to keep the aliens away. This wolf was not amused in the least. Fortunately, it was on secondary double glazing and has not done a great deal of harm, but he can't stay here if he is going to damage the place, and he could have set a real fire. He is going to the doctor tomorrow. It is a pity there are no longer places where he could dry out in a mental hospital.

He has gone back to his lodgings just up the road. I have told him he is welcome to come here during the day if he is stone cold sober, but otherwise to keep away. I don't want to see him then. The doctor has arranged for a psychiatric social worker to visit him regularly.

Will seems to have accepted these new arrangements, shared kitchen, bathroom and washing machine and the geraniums are doing really well. He comes down most days now it is summer and has even taken on an allotment down below in what used to be part of my Dad's garden. When he is well he is very well and works like fury all day, but only lasts a few weeks and he disappears into his bed again for a week and emerges a sadder and a wiser man. Even when he is not drinking he has developed a bit of a lurch along and these absences when he goes all glazed for a few seconds are becoming more frequent. I keep telling him to pace himself and take things more steadily but it doesn't seem to make a lot of difference.

He collapsed in the bottom garden today, and by the time I got home my neighbour had called an ambulance and they took him to hospital. They tested his heart and found nothing wrong. He actually reminds me of some of the epileptics I met at work, but I suppose the doctors would have thought of that if they took a history, or if he told them much.

I'm glad that he has decided to give Ann his car, or at least let her have it on permanent loan, as she can't afford her own and with three small children it will be a great help. I wouldn't like him to be on the roads now. To think that it is only six months since we were in Australia and he was so fit!

I'm going on holiday with my girlfriends from the Art Club. I shall leave the house all locked up and the keys with my parents. It will be such a relief to get away from everything, and not to worry about the house, Will, or anything.

It was a great holiday, full of laughs and without any men to pander to or worry about. Even the 'girls' who are still married felt the same. We were a group of eight ladies of a certain age, and we all got on well together and generally fell in with each other's plans for the day. Some were early risers and got up early for a walk, while the rest of us grabbed an extra hour. We all just got on with each other and modified our own ideas to fit in with others. I have even learned to drink red wine instead of white and to find that gin and tonic is bearable if there is nothing else. I drew the line at Greek dancing though as I am still wary of my ankle.

When things went wrong, like power failures, we just laughed. It would have been a major drama for most husbands. I look forward to going again next year.

Back to the usual drama at home. Will had a fall in the street and dislocated his shoulder. Two young men picked him up and saw him back to his lodgings so of course he didn't go to the doctor. By the time I found out about it, he had a permanent injury to his shoulder as it could not be manipulated back into place. Now he is complaining that he cannot do what he wants to, as he has no power in that arm and I think he is ashamed of the way it droops. The cure for a crippled shoulder is, you guess…I haven't seen him for a week or two so he is having a real binge this time.

My conscience got the better of me and I went to his bedsit and beat on the door. Talk about a wreck of a man! He looked terrible. He had carried on drinking until he was too ill to go out and get any more and then went through cold turkey. I've seen him do this many times, but it must have been really bad this time. He has asked to 'come home' for a few days so I'll let him have the settee until I've managed to get him eating properly again. He will have to go back to his own place at the weekend, as I am going away again to stay with Ann, bed or no bed. Things haven't improved down there and she sounds at the end of her tether. Why did she have to marry a drunkard too?

Things are really bad. At least, he slept on the sofa and let me share the bed with Ann, but that is all I can say for him. The poor kids have no kind of a father, and I had to go food shopping as soon as I got there as there was nothing to eat in the house. Several bottles of beer though, littering up the fridge.

I took the kids out to allow Ann to grab a couple of hours sleep in the afternoon. I felt bad about coming back and leaving them, but I have a meeting on Monday. It is not as if he doesn't earn good money, though Ann doesn't see much of it. She is even washing up at a pub to try to make ends meet.

It is a good job that my parents are keeping well for their age as they cause me no trouble. I still have to keep a beady eye on Will. He lasts for about a month, fit as a flea and brown as a berry with all the time in the gardens, then he seems to hit a wall of depression. You can really see it coming on and the next thing I know, he is drinking again and has slunk off to his lair.

It usually coincides with a visit I make to the girls. They reckon, he does it deliberately to get my attention focussed back on him. I'll give him focus! I've got a spare key to his room now so that I can go and drag him out of bed before he gets too far sunk into the drinking. Otherwise, he goes on until he makes himself ill again. So long as I can keep him busy, he gets over it fairly rapidly. I shall have to get him to the doctor somehow.

Ann has thrown her husband out. She found some drugs in his toolbox and then he attacked her and she called the police. Good for her! She can do without that and will be better off financially and emotionally as a single mother. He has never acted as a proper father to those children, and now, he is prepared to use them as a weapon to hurt their mother. It's emotional blackmail, but he will find that he has all her family and friends against him. I shall be down there at the weekend, if not before. She is a bit frightened about what he will do now. At least Will was never violent.

He even offered to come down with me if that would have been helpful, but I thought that Ann would have enough to cope with at this time. I'm going down for as long as she needs me. Will has phoned and offered his support and any help she requires. The most important thing has been his car as at least she is not confined to the house with a young child while the others are at school. I'm glad I persuaded him to get a phone in his bedsit, though it is a bit of a mixed blessing as he rings me several times a day to keep in touch.

At last, I can go back and get on with my business now that things have settled down a bit and, apart from the legal wrangles and debts he left her with, Ann is feeling safer. She is really thin and taking anti-depressants, but she has a real reason for them. Jane has rallied round and offered support, but she is back at work now and worried about child-minding for her little one.

Will has booked a holiday for us in the autumn. I thought it would be a good idea to take his mind off other things, and I will have something to look forward to. I am going to take Ann away for a week in a caravan in the summer holidays. I think the children will like that, and perhaps the break will do her good. She is worried about her husband getting into the house while she isn't there, but I think that he has got the message, and there is virtually nothing that he has ever contributed to the home that he could claim. He has done a lot of carpentry work with timber from his workplace, but there are an awful lot of unfinished jobs. We have taken some 'before' photos, just in case he does any damage.

My goodness, those children are traumatised by the ill feeling heaped on their mother by their father. It took a long time to get them relaxed and the little boy is still very insecure. We had a good holiday on the whole and they ate well and had some fun, but they don't want to move far from their mother. Ann looks well, all slim, but her self-esteem has had a battering for a long time. Still the only way is up and she knows that we shall not let her go under.

I got back to find Will in hospital. Apparently, he fell down the stairs at his lodge, crashed into a radiator with his bad shoulder and did it no good at all. He swears he wasn't drinking. He has seen a specialist and had some tests. I'll take him for his appointment in a couple of weeks.

They have diagnosed epilepsy and have given him some drugs to combat it. The trick now is to get him to look after himself so that they can do their job. He needs to eat regularly and not drink. This is going to be difficult because his bad shoulder prevents him from getting stuck into the garden, and he gets tired very easily. You can just see the frustration building up. I can't be watching him all the time, what about the jobs I am trying to do and the need to spend as much time with Ann as I can. I am the ultimate deterrent for the children when they play her up. "Just you wait 'til I tell your Granny what you have done!" It is a good thing that they know I love them dearly, but also that I won't have them being cheeky to their mother. She is having enough difficulty in hanging on to her self-respect. Aren't men buggers!

Will is trying hard to stick to the rules, but he is looking a much sicker man. He has booked a fantastic cruise for November, but I keep telling him that I won't go unless he stays away from the booze. I think I would even go without him, and that is an option too.

Ann has got a preliminary hearing for her divorce. That is not a problem. What is going to happen to her children is. She is terrified that she will not get full custody of them, even though that waster has not got a proper home and is living in an old caravan so that his creditors can't catch up with him. At least he has moved out of the garage where he took up residence at first. What chance of child support? That is a real joke. Good thing that her father and I can come up with some handouts. That is one thing about Will. He truly loves his daughters and would never see them short. She wouldn't dream of asking for anything though.

Chapter Twenty
Ups and Downs

I am so excited about this holiday, travelling from Singapore to Penang and across to India. We have even booked the extension to visit the Taj Mahal. You can't go all that way and miss that out! I do hope that Will will be alright. He is going to take a stick to help with the walking, but I can't see him swimming with that crippled shoulder. If determination will take him there, he will be fine. I have been buying clothes for months so will have a whole new wardrobe. The only thing I haven't got is an evening dress as I have got too fat for all the ones I used to wear. I bought Will a white DJ so at least he will look the part. I think I shall have to make a dress as all the ones in the shops are polyester and I remember passing out in Hong Kong, so I need a cotton one. One person in danger of passing out is enough!

A wonderful holiday again, though we had to be very wary about getting overtired – no late night jollifications, and I bet we had the smallest bar bill on board. I was the one who went sick. I must have eaten something I was allergic to, and I was really poorly for a couple of days but fortunately, it was while we were at sea and I didn't miss anything.

I was so glad we went to the Taj but a little sad. It is a monument to a great love and very atmospheric but I had some sadness about the love we have lost because of the booze. I can never really trust him anymore. I always seem to be on my guard, watching and waiting to pre-empt the next fall from grace.

Will was full of it and thoroughly enjoyed showing me all the places he had visited with the Navy. I'm sure I managed to hide my misgivings.

Now we are back, he has gone to his lodgings again as real life has kicked in and I am off down to see the children.

He couldn't keep it up, despite his good intentions and promises. Life cannot be a holiday all the time, though he has booked another cruise for next year.

I haven't seen him for some time, in fact, not since I came back from the girls. I suppose I had better go to his bedsit to see that he is alright. I have a key to the street door even if not to his room. I suppose the delay in opening the door gives him time to hide the bottles.

What a good thing I went. He was completely out of his mind with jaundice, sitting with the door open, 'waiting for the maid to bring him some lunch'. Goodness knows how long he has been like this. The place was a tip and there were several empty bottles under the sink. He was completely oblivious to what was going on and didn't even know I was there. I found the phone and called the doctor who came and packed him off to hospital. By the time I had gathered his belongings and followed in the car, he was on a drip and I was told that I had just found him in time as he was very poorly.

Well, he has come through this time. He was in hospital for three weeks. They told him that he really must stop drinking. His liver is in a bad way but will improve if he lays off alcohol entirely, but his brain is permanently damaged. He is very remorseful and promises not to touch another drop. I wish I could believe it. Anyway, he knows that he dare not drink in my house and he is staying for a week or so, but I dare not leave him alone when I go to visit the girls. I don't want any more damage.

I discovered what they meant by brain damage today. It is about a fortnight since he had his last drinking spree. No, it didn't last.

I know he hasn't been drinking again for I read him the riot act and he knows he is not welcome down here if he so much as sniffs a wine gum! He is still a bit shaky on his feet. I would watch him suddenly go vague and he would have fallen several times if I hadn't held on to him. Anyway, I went up to his bedsit with some shopping and we were sitting talking in front of the big window. Suddenly, I saw a lightning flash in the distance and then Will was rolling on the floor with a proper grand mal

155

epileptic fit. He was out for about 20 minutes after the fitting, the jerking and eye-rolling, turning blue and foaming at the mouth had subsided. I blessed the fact that he had a phone in his room now, and I didn't have to leave him to call for a doctor. It was very frightening for me as I could do nothing but make him comfortable on the floor after the fitting had ended. He was still out for the count but breathing more easily when the doctor came. It was a lady doctor who said straight away that alcohol had caused the fit. I said he hadn't had any for about a fortnight, and she explained that the withdrawal had caused the fit. The lightning might have been a trigger too. So off he went in the ambulance to the other hospital. We have two in our area, one dealt with his gastric problems and the other with his head. I followed and saw him settled, but he only stayed a while as he had only had one major fit and they confirmed the diagnosis and made a forward appointment with the specialist. The other absences are part of the same trouble, but if he stays off the booze and takes anti-convulsive tablets, it should come under control. If only!

This time he was firmly told to hand in his driving licence. I'm so glad we persuaded him to hand over his car to Ann last year.

What they didn't allow for is the depression he is suffering from and that he feels no longer in control of his life. What is his cure for depression? You guessed. Drink himself stupid, forget his pills and have another fit. It is almost like a deliberate self-destruct. The last time they tried treating him for depression he didn't take the pills because he knew he couldn't drink. He is on such a cocktail of chemicals now that it is even more important that he takes them regularly and eats as well. I have him down for lunch each day to try to ensure that he has one good meal, even though he is perfectly capable of cooking for himself. A better cook than I am if he wants to be – on a good day. The moment I turn my back, like when I took Ann and the children on holiday, he is back to the old routine. It is deliberate attention seeking. I am fed up!

Soon be holiday time again. I'm almost dreading it. I keep telling him that if he doesn't look after himself, I'm not going. I hope I don't have to carry that threat out as I've never been on a safari, but honestly it will be no rest cure.

It is for all the world like taking a handicapped child on holiday. Clutching a stick and my hand we left the airport. I also had the two flight bags: my handbag and the camera to carry. The transport to the hotel had gone without us. Fortunately, a helpful car-hire man took pity on us, rang the hotel and called a taxi. I was moderately fraught by the time we reached the hotel, and we were late for the briefing meeting. The next day, there was to be a tour of Nairobi by minibus. Will cracked his head on the door getting in, bled streams and instead of a tour of the town we had to go to the local hospital. They were very good, though you had to pay up-front. Will was bandaged and given a turban of tubigrip which made him look like a Sunday roast. Lots of people enquired about him as he had created quite a stir while everyone was waiting to board the minibuses. He just looked a bit soft. Maybe it was the concussion, or maybe the effects of the long flight and stopping drinking a few days earlier. Whatever, it was hardly a hopeful start to an action packed holiday.

The driver who took us to hospital adopted us into his group and we were fortunate with our companions, two American couples who seemed to be on the same wavelength as we were and we got on really well. Apart from his turban, Will seemed okay and we set off sitting in the middle of the bus for the first leg. We agreed to swap seats daily as the back seat tended to be a lot bumpier so everyone would have a turn there. The driver turned out to be a great guy. He was a big fellow from the Kikuyu tribe and, obviously, a very experienced guide with a good sense of humour. We headed out of town on a reasonable road that soon deteriorated into a mass of potholes. I was glad to have such a good driver as we went past lots of broken-down and stuck vehicles which had failed to negotiate the potholes and the mud.

We stopped at the Equator for a water demonstration to prove that it drained one way north of the equator and the opposite way when we were south of it, within a few feet.

When we reached our campsite, twin bedded tents with all mod cons, we went out for our first game drive.

I can't begin to describe all we saw on that four-day safari. It was truly wonderful and I was so glad that we went. After the poor start, Will recovered and was almost his old self, happy, sociable and focussed. He tired easily but wouldn't admit to it, and, of course, the antibiotics he was taking was the civilised excuse for alcohol avoidance. We were both pretty tired by the time the safari ended and the cruise began. I hoped for good photos, for there is little chance of repeating the experience. I should have lots of material for paintings.

The cruise took us on a circular tour leading to the Seychelles. I was not impressed by several islands we visited, either tourist traps or with an indifferent population. I was looking forward to revisiting the Seychelles. Just as we reached there, the drought broke and the stormy skies gave an entirely different aspect to the familiar beaches. There has been a great deal of change in the last ten years, not all of it for the better, but I suppose the same could be said of us.

I for one returned refreshed in mind and spirit and plunged into preparations for Christmas and everything. Will suffered from anti-climax. Jane did her best to provide a diversion with a new baby and then her husband broke his leg playing football. Talk about change!

I went down to stay with Ann and see the new arrival. Will went to ground in his bedsit. Christmas came. It wasn't very jolly. One year I shall go away from it all. The expense and heartache of running a one-woman show is hardly worth it.

My parents came for dinner and the girls came up later to eat up the leftovers and to bring the new baby to show my parents. Although Will put in an appearance, he was obviously in the middle of a drinking session and couldn't do justice to his food. He will be better when he can get out into the garden again.

I've given up trying to be a consultant. Not that we have had a lot of work lately. We have been bidding for jobs in the last few months, but there doesn't seem to be a lot of work around, and I really can't concentrate on much outside my home. I have to spend more time with my parents to see that they eat properly. Dad is ill, and Mum is wearing herself out, trying to wait on him and keep an eye on him. He has keeled over in the garden a couple of times, but unlike others I could mention, he just gets on with things.

Will is better again now that there is gardening to be done, but I have to keep on to him to pace himself and not get overtired. He works like fury for several days and then feels ill for a week and begins to look around for the cure. He is frustrated that he cannot do the things he could as a young man. It would help if he would make sure he has regular meals as with all the tablets he is taking he needs to eat properly.

Ann has decided that she wants to go in for nursing and she is going to start an access course at the local college in September. I'm pleased that she has found a proper career direction as I'm sure she will make a wonderful nurse. It will be tough going to complete the course as a single mother, though I will give her all the support I can. That is another reason for making no outside commitments.

Will has been given notice to leave his bedsit. Apparently, his landlady is putting it up for sale, not just that he has caused so much damage with his drinking bouts. I've told him to look for somewhere else and to get his name on the council list. He may be lucky with all the medical problems he has. I suppose, I shall have to offer him accommodation as a temporary measure, conditional upon no drinking of course. I really don't fancy sharing my space with him. It has been good to be able to send him home when I have had enough. He is not exactly scintillating company.

It really cannot be for long as I shall have to persuade Mum and Dad to come and stay. Dad is really bad now, just hanging on with the help of frequent blood transfusions. Despite it all, he is the best patient in the world. Even when the young doctors can't raise a vein to get a line in, he tells them to have another go. And he does everything he is told, not like another I could mention.

Will has booked one last cruise to the Black Sea. It should be less hectic than the others and with Will under my eye before we go at least he will not be suffering from cold turkey. I could manage to forego this one so he knows I shall not go if he falls from grace.

It was a close run thing but at least we got away without me having to half carry him to the airport. It was as near as I've got to relaxing for some time, despite the excursions and sightseeing. Will enjoyed it all and we saw places and did things that would normally not be possible. We have even won frequent cruiser awards, though I think they will be the last. He seems totally to forget that we are divorced and is making plans for what he will do for my house in the future. I grind my teeth mainly and smile weakly.

I've given up hope that things will ever get better; I think that his health has got so bad that the doctors were right when they said that his brain will never recover. When he begins to get overtired his balance goes, and he begins to slur his speech even though he has not been anywhere near a bottle. It is even worse to be taken for a drunk when you haven't been drinking.

Chapter Twenty-One
Apart

I enjoyed the cruise and we saw things that I certainly never would have visited on my own, but I am glad to get back to see how Mum is coping with Dad. It is wearing her out even though he tries to be very good. It is nearly time they came to me and made use of the rooms I had designed for them. I shall go away on this holiday to Provence with my friends but after that I shall have to persuade them.

We are OK for the holiday. Whew! We booked nearly a year ago, and I am taking some of us in my car so I can't back out. It will be the last time I shall be able to get away with my Art Club friends for some time and the trip through France is an important part of the holiday. It will be a giggle as we always have fun together. We are staying in an old farmhouse in Provence. We may possibly do some painting but probably more chatting over a glass of wine after driving is finished of course. I have arranged for Ann to come up and to keep an eye on Mum and Dad at weekends. Her children will be staying with their dad in that rotten old caravan.

I wish I could trust Will to keep an eye on things but I'd be worried about the house, let alone my parents. Part of his balance problem is real giddiness but tablets soaked in vodka are not very effective. He has switched to vodka because he thinks I won't notice it but I have had so much practice in watching his every mood that I always spot it. He is now seeing the doctor on a regular basis but the perishing man has only told him to cut down, not give up entirely. If he had only done what I asked, Will would have accepted the order of a commanding officer and packed it in like he did smoking. An alcoholic can't "cut down" it is either self-destruct or nothing. He probably does not admit to how much he drinks anyway.

Even a small drink will set him off on a bender, and he knows how ill it will make him.

Well that is that. He was picked up off the street and taken to a hospital. The doctor there said it was drinking that caused it and any breakthrough fits he may have are probably if he has not taken his tablets regularly because of the drinking or can also be part of the withdrawal symptoms that kick in about two weeks after his last drink. He really can't win with this. When he has recovered from cold turkey this time, he can find a new home. I am fed up to the back teeth at spending my sympathy on somebody who deliberately makes himself ill. He knows the effect it has on him so why does he do it again and again and again? I am not having him back here when they discharge him. He has had his last chance.

When they discharged him, he caught a train to Cheltenham and stayed in some bed-and-breakfast place there. I suppose he thought I would take pity on him. Well he is wrong. It is time for the tough love routine. I have been too soft.

He has found another bed-and-breakfast place in town. Oh well. I am off to France.

Oh the bliss of a holiday without men! We have had a thoroughly lovely time, spoilt only by the prospect of returning. It was great to be in the warmth and the sunshine. Even when it rained, we could make a joke of it. It is back to reality now. I have a garden to sort out now that my gardener has gone on strike. I confidently expect he will be asked to leave his lodgings soon, as I saw him up town, looking very much the worse for wear. I am quite ashamed to be associated with him. I know he is not my problem, but he is an embarrassment. Why can't the doctor send him to a place to dry out? I found a place a few months ago when he said he was desperate to get better, but when he phoned and they said it cost £2,000 a week, he lost interest. Such a shame as he might even have made a start on the counselling that is long overdue and might even get to the root cause of all his problems. It would have been worth it for the state of his health, but he is probably too far-gone now.

He has been thrown out of his lodgings and came whining to me 'to come home'. I gave him the settee for the night and then took him to the railway station. I have enough to worry about with Mum and Dad without him too. They will have to

162

come here soon. I go up every day to make sure they are eating. Mum is fading away, let alone Dad, but he is adamant that he will not come here while Will is around.

I had a phone call from the Lake District. That is where he finally came to his senses. He doesn't know why he went there as he doesn't know anyone. Now he thinks he is too far away, and he is going to come closer. Apparently, he found himself sitting on a park bench talking to a down-and-out and realised that was where he was heading. At least, he is still alive.

I have had more phone calls from Gloucester and Cardiff so he is getting closer, wandering around and seeing the sights. Stone cold sober by the sound of it. Well, I can't have him here.

He has finally fetched up a few miles away. Apparently, that was the nearest bed-and-breakfast place, in a pub. However, he has been to the doctor by bus and has been referred to counselling, at last. The only trouble is that it is in the evenings and there are no buses from where he is to the hospital. I suppose I shall have to take him. After all, he has finally done what I was urging all those years. It is only once a week and it is surely worth trying. He needs to get to the root cause of his alcohol dependency.

Mum and Dad have moved in with me and Mum is beginning to get some rest. Dad is hanging on until Christmas by sheer willpower. He looks ghastly now and they cannot give him any more transfusions. It is the beginning of the end.

Will is enjoying his counselling sessions and in particular they have been discussing his experiences during the war. I thought that had a lot to do with his problem and really the Service should have picked up on that before he retired. It might have saved him, and us, ten years of misery. He tells me a bit about it as I take him back to the pub. He doesn't seem at all inclined to drink. Perhaps he has come to realise that to be a real man you can run on coke or lemonade and lime like Dad learned to after his hepatitis.

Dad is worse and I can't really leave the old folks for even a couple of hours so I shall not be able to run taxi service to the counselling sessions. Will will have to get a proper taxi but I bet that will be too difficult. At least, it has meant that he sees me once a week. I shall have to look out for somewhere else for him to live.

I popped in to the Art Club for a couple of minutes and was having a bleat. Brian, bless his heart, offered Will a room at his house which is just down the road. It takes one to know one and Brian is also an alcoholic though, supposedly, reformed at present. Anyway, it is a lifeline at present.

I did suggest to Dad that Will could move into their cottage now that they are living with me, but he blew a fuse. He saw what happened to my house when the wolves were around. Besides, Will is on the waiting list for a council flat, so staying with a friend is better than occupying an empty house.

The day after Will moved in down the road, Brian was rushed into hospital with a chest infection and Will was left with his dogs and a filthy house. He is having a real blitz as it was crawling. Brian has been bad with his chest, depression and drink for a long time so he hasn't been able to do much. I think that Will has taken that as a warning of how things bad things can become. The counselling is having a halo effect and he is very scathing about drinkers who cannot give up. He hasn't made his way to the hospital under his own steam though but perhaps it is closed for Christmas. Having a project to get on with is really doing him good and Brian won't recognise his home when he gets back.

Christmas time and Dad achieved his ambition to celebrate their 70th wedding anniversary together on Christmas Eve. There was a nice article in the local paper and his friend who is mayor this year came to visit, complete with his chain of office, so that pleased Mum. He struggled out of bed to join us for Christmas dinner but could scarcely eat a thing. It was only Mum, Dad, Will and me that day but the girls are coming up for Mum's birthday and will help with the leftovers. They are not bringing the grandchildren this year as Dad looks so ghastly that I would rather they remember him as he was a few months ago. I am sleeping at the foot of his bed now in case he needs help in the night. He is very stoic and will not ask for help, but I would rather be there. It will not be long now.

Dad died today. There is lots to do even though he wrote out all his instructions. Mum is a bit vague. I hope she will be alright. Will is still at Brian's.

It was just the close family for the cremation. Will was very good with Ann who was terribly upset. Dad didn't want a fuss for Mum's sake, but she is being marvellous. We shall have a memorial service in a few weeks' time when I can get it organised. We owe it to the town to have a proper send-off as he was involved in so much.

That was a funeral too far for Will, and he has gone walkabout as he couldn't face it. All of his good intentions out of the window. Not my concern. Mum was fine and the grandchildren got some idea of just what their "Pamp" had achieved. I feel that he has now been properly laid to rest.

Mum will not be going home again now that I have her under my wing. I couldn't imagine her on her own and neither could she. Neither of us would have had a moment's rest. She is pretty easy company here and keeps Will at bay. He came back to Brian's and is still busy keeping house for him. Together they seem to rub along.

Great news! A flat has come up and with all his medical problems to the fore, it is well situated on the ground floor and will be adapted for his needs. We shall have more than enough to furnish it from my parents' home

He is really thrilled to have a place of his own, failing mine, of course. We have ordered carpets and found a bed advertised locally. Apart from that he had all the furniture he needed and some to spare. There is a grab handle over the bath and one outside the front door but apart from that it is a commodious ground floor flat with a kitchen as big as mine. We have ordered a cooker but he has Mum's fridge, washing machine, spinner and two kettles, hoovers and irons, a table cover for ironing, bed linen, cushions etc., etc. he has already been busy with the polish and it is good to see him take a pride in his new home. It is about a 15-minute walk from mine so just about right.

I have just found the problem with the flat. The local shop is an off-licence. As soon as he began to feel lonely, he was off for some consolation and there was a burbling great heap on the end of the phone. It is such a shame, as he really set out with such good intentions to keep sober. Anyway, I have told him that he is not welcome here unless he is stone cold sober, so if he wants to see us, he will have to stay sober. It would terrify Mum if he came here drunk. She is very fearful these days. I suppose it is only to be expected. Apart from that she looks well and is eating properly.

I couldn't raise him when I rang to ask if he needed any shopping. I haven't seen him for a week so I called round. He was sober, but ill. Apparently, he carried on drinking until he passed out and wasn't capable of going to the shop to get any more. Then, he had to go through the cold turkey stage and since he hadn't been eating or taking his pills he has started having fits again. I chewed him off. Picked up the debris and got him some milk to drink as his stomach will not take real food yet.

His pristine flat is a tip. It didn't take long to do that. The carpet is stained with pee and spilt food and he had wrecked his radio. He was very apologetic, abjectly ashamed of himself and promising that he will never, never… We'll see. I felt sorry for him and told him he could come for Sunday lunch if he could get fit enough again. He has five days to do it. He may manage to pull himself together.

He got here. Goodness knows how, as he was still very shaky and had to use his stick to walk. He couldn't eat much of his dinner, but he tried hard to hold a conversation with Mum and to pretend that all was well. I took pity on him and gave him a ride home in the car after lunch. He has tried to clean up his flat and had all his bedding soaking in the bath. He has to see the doctor on Friday so he will keep sober until then. It is still like "captain's rounds" – stand to attention, swear all is well and everything in order, then collapse in a big heap after. If only he would come clean with the doctor and admit just how much he is drinking, but he can't do that. I doubt if he really knows as he can't even remember what he has been doing. It is as if a black cloud descends on him and he runs on automatic to press the self-destruct button.

I am going down to see the children this weekend. I have got a granny-sitter for the day.'

**

Liz went to see the girls at the weekend. She had a friend to 'granny-sit' so that she could get away. She was singing in the car, happy to have a day off, free from stress if only for a few hours. There was still the responsibility even though her mother was really no problem as she spent most of her time sitting and dozing. When the weather was suitable, Will would turn up most days to do a bit in the garden, but he was getting less and less steady on his feet. Liz spent quite a time talking to him, as he was lonely in his flat despite having all his music and television and films. He said 'good day' to some of the neighbours and moaned about the behaviour of those upstairs, but he had no real friends. Most of the people around there had known each other for years, and he was still a new-comer to the town. Liz still wished that the shop was not so close, as she was sure that he still went to get some booze as soon as he left her home. He often sounded slurry if he rang in the evening.

The specialist increased his epilepsy tablets at his annual review, but Liz was beginning to wonder if they were having an adverse effect on him when he was sober and tired out by the evening, or whether he was still trying to drink despite the increased tablets. The girls were convinced that it was drinking, but Liz was inclined to think that the tablets were having an effect, particularly, on his balance. He was beginning to get the shakes and having trouble feeding himself as well as his balance problem. The trouble was that if he was drinking, he did not take the tablets properly and did not eat regularly or he would take the whole cocktail of chemicals on an empty stomach and be completely shot away.

Whatever it was, caring for granny was a lot less bother.

Liz found him collapsed at home again. She was unable to help him up from the floor as he must have weighed around 20 stones. He had to back himself up to the settee and somehow raise himself until he could slide onto the seat. It looked very painful with that dislocated shoulder, and it left him exhausted. Everything was smelling of urine, as he had peed himself with the fit and he was very disoriented. She wasn't allowed to call the doctor, though if only he had seen him in that state, he might have abandoned the 'There, there, try not to drink so much' approach. If only he knew him better. It was not just a drink he fancied, but the whole bottle or more until he would keel over. He tried to hide the evidence sometimes, but the presence of a lemonade bottle was enough to tell Liz what was happening.

At least, it didn't upset her so much. She tried to address the problem as the addiction, not the person, and so didn't feel so let down. She didn't like it but tried not to take it as a personal affront that booze was more important than her feelings and despite everything she still tried to help him, for there was really nobody else. She no longer kept quiet about it and would talk about it to her friends. Bottling it up only made her feel a failure herself, and she couldn't let it destroy her as well as him. That was why she had left him so many years earlier.

He would always be welcome at her home but only if he was stone, cold sober so that he would not frighten her mother.

Will too knew that the only one who could stop it was himself, but that it wasn't easy. At least, he admitted there was a problem. When he was sober once more, he would be sad about what had happened again. He was becoming very emotional about what he was doing to himself, but hadn't yet found the way to stop.

Liz was so concerned about Will's deteriorating health that she even had a word with his doctor about his exhaustion after a short walk even when he was completely sober. His drinking habits were such that he only stopped when he had made himself too weak to walk to the shop, and then he put himself through the strain of cold turkey. It must have been a tremendous strain on his system. Even when he had appeared for Sunday lunch and that meant he was sober, Liz found that the walk home with her support was almost too much for him, and he was really shaky and utterly exhausted when they reached the flat.

He would stay sober for a few weeks and then the black cloud would descend upon him again. He would burble on the phone for a couple of days and then it would go quiet, as he had reached the stage of being unable to walk to the shop and would suffer cold turkey once again. It must have been a terrible stress on his system time after time and only a strong person could survive all that. Just fancy, still craving alcohol when you know what it is going to do to you.

The doctor referred him for a heart scan in case the alcohol had affected his heart and as Liz said, it showed he still had a heart but he had some signs of damage which might account for the exhaustion and shortness of breath.

He was also referred for an endoscopy. This appointment referred back to his admission for jaundice a long time previously. Liz decided to get a granny-sitter so that she could take him.

In the meanwhile, Ann finished her nursing course and got a part time job in the field she wanted. This enabled her to both work and get some state support so that was a burden lifted from Liz. She seemed to have been juggling the family as well as having to worry about with Will's health problems. He was usually there to listen to her worries about the family and always ready to offer financial support, but she could have done with more practical support so she could go and see them more.

The endoscope revealed oesophageal varices, that is, veins in the throat that could cause him to bleed to death if they were to rupture. Not a happy scenario. The only answer was absolutely no drinking. Yet again. He also had to take some more tablets to lower the pressure in the veins.

Nurse friends told Liz lurid stories of patients bleeding to death, and there was even a programme on the television that reinforced that scenario. Liz told Will to frighten him into doing the right thing, and they also agreed to get a cleaner to help him keep the flat in good order, provided he didn't drink and put her off. He also agreed to get meals on wheels to ensure that he had proper meals.

He wasn't able to walk as far as Liz's home now so she agreed to pick him up on Sundays and to take him shopping twice a week. He quite enjoyed pottering around using a 'zimmer-trolley'. Together with the cleaner, at least, he would see someone most days. Liz hoped this would keep the black cloud at bay.

***

There are still some times when the burbling over the phone indicated that he has been drinking again. I could not imagine how he got the booze since he had such problems with walking and balance, but my friends reported seeing him coming out of the off-licence early in the morning or on the bus to the town centre.

He must be pretty determined to make that effort and for what? It only makes him ill again.

When he has drunk enough, he keels over and falls to the floor and then when he has gathered his senses, makes all that effort to get back into the chair. If ever I found him like that, I make an all-out bottle search and pour anything remaining down the sink. If he is still on the floor I cover him up until he is able to drag himself up onto the chair. I tell him what a b…fool he was, but he is well aware of that himself and it doesn't seem to make any difference when the mood is upon him.

One of these days, I am afraid he just will not recover.

Today, when I went to take him shopping, I found him in the bath, stuck and unable to get out again. How embarrassing! Whatever had made him want to have a bath when he could scarcely get up off the floor was a mystery. No doubt it had seemed like a good idea at the time. Usually, he has a shower when he comes to mine for lunch on a Sunday.

He refused to let me call the ambulance service and said he would try to get out whilst I went shopping. I put a towel around him for he was cold and exhausted by the efforts he had made already. When I got back, he was able to see reason and let me make the call. I made a point of stressing his weight and medical conditions and waited to see who would turn up. The ambulance brought two young girl paramedics who had no hope of moving him but had brought back up of the fire engine and some hefty firefighters. It took four of them to heave him out and then the girls gave him oxygen as he was exhausted by his efforts. I persuaded them to leave him in his own bed and he promised never to take a bath again!

This time, he has walked into a car. It was parked at the time, but he walked across the road and fell into it. The neighbours called the ambulance, but he only got as far as the local hospital to be patched up, and they called me to collect him. It was a good thing that they didn't take him off to one of the regional hospitals, as they would not have known to contact me about him. He had no recollection of why he was out, but it was probably to visit the off-licence again. On the other hand, even when sober, he suffers from the shakes now, almost like Parkinson's, and he gets exhausted just sitting up in his chair all the morning. I wonder about the tablets again. He is certainly a very sick man, and I am pleased that they have arranged for him to go to the day hospital twice a week where he can have a bath and the local doctor can keep an eye on him. He will also get a meal and some company.

The school holidays are upon us, and my grandchildren are coming up for a time. I can no longer leave my mother to visit them but the children were quite happy to come to granny's house because they know they will get spoiled. They aren't a lot of bother and I have arranged to have granny-sitters so that I can take them out for half a day to visit wild-life parks, and I feed them their favourite foods, let them have their favourite TV programmes and generally we get on well. I will also take them to see their grandfather if he is alright. I go in first to check that he is on his best behaviour. Our daughters would be mortified if the children found him splatted. He loves to see them, but doesn't really know how to hold a conversation with them and has to be prompted. If he is not good, I send them to the swings until I have got him sorted.

The holidays were a bit difficult this time. I called in to collect Will for Sunday lunch and found him on the floor again. I went around, looking for bottles and made him comfortable, with the phone nearby. Later when I rang, there was no response, so I went down to his flat again. He was still on the floor, unable to get up, so I brought him a jug of water, put the phone within reach and made sure that he was warm and left him to sober up. He has done cold turkey often enough, so this was nothing unusual, but normally, he managed to get into bed within 24 hours. The next day, he was still on the floor, but wouldn't let me call an ambulance. That is the trouble with being an 'ex', I can only do what he wants. He was sober by then and had got over the shakes, but still hadn't found the strength to heave himself up off the floor. I tried to make him promise that he would call for help if he felt any worse, but was told that he would please himself.

The next thing I knew, the following day, was a phone call from the hospital in Bath to say that he had been brought in by ambulance and had been admitted. The driver from the day-hospital had called to collect him and when there was no reply, he had peered through the letterbox and saw him on the floor so he called the housing association manager to unlock the door.

So today, instead of taking the children out for the day, I've had to gather up supplies and go down to Bath. I left them in the car while I went in to see what the situation was. He was on the ward where they usually had alcoholics to dry out. He looked really rough, but when I brought in the children in he was able to talk to them while I went in search of the ward sister.

"Did you know about all his medical conditions?" I started, because of course the town where I live is shared by two regional hospitals and the one in Bath had no record of his treatment for epilepsy. The sister thought she knew it all because she had lots of alcoholics to deal with. She didn't listen when I told her that he had already got sober by going through cold turkey and that his problem had been exhaustion after that episode. She looked at me as if I was talking non-sense and told me that it wasn't so because he still had the shakes. She didn't want to know about the effect of his epilepsy tablets because it was not on the notes at that hospital. Of course, it wasn't, he was being treated for that at the other. I found that they were giving him the standard drying-out treatment because of his symptoms even though by the time he had reached there he was sober. He had never been given drugs before, and I was really worried about the effects he might suffer because of his other conditions.

I might just as well have saved my breath, as the sister took not a bit of notice of what I was saying, as they were accustomed to dealing with alcoholics on the ward, and she just didn't want to hear anything else.

I collected the children and promised to come down again later. We went to IKEA where the children could have a good look around and a special meal so the day was not entirely wasted even though I had used up my granny-sitter. The round trip to Bath was more than 50 miles, not as if it was just around the corner.

Fortunately, another friend was able to come in and take care of them all for the evening, so after tea, I went down to the hospital again, hoping to have more sense from the night nurse team.

Will looked really awful. *He looks as if he is dying*, I thought and went straight away and buttonholed the nurse and asked exactly what treatment he was receiving.

"It is the standard detox treatment, with lithium to relieve the symptoms," she said.

"But he had already sobered up before they called the ambulance. He just couldn't find the strength to get up off the floor!"

She assured me that it was not so because he had the shakes.

"Didn't I tell the sister this afternoon that he is being treated for epilepsy and this has given him a kind of Parkinsonian tremor? He is always shaky and has difficulty walking and feeding himself!"

"There is nothing in his notes here about that," she replied.

"He is being treated in Swindon for the epilepsy. That's why I made a point of telling the sister this afternoon. I am his next of kin, you'll find that on the records, so that is why I made a point of telling you that the treatment you are giving him is not appropriate, as he had already sobered up and he has never had drugs to help him do it."

No wonder he looked so ghastly. He could scarcely open his eyes to see I was there, let alone raise a smile. He had deteriorated so much since the morning. I took away his dirty clothes but reminded the nurse that I would not be able to get there for another three days, as it was too long a journey, and I had other responsibilities.

I went home, had another day with the children and the following day, I took them back home. Not much of a week's holiday for them.

I took one morning to recover, then, armed with the clean washing, I got a granny-sitter and went to Bath. This time, I found a nurse who seemed to be more switched on. Will still looked awful, almost as if he had had a stroke, flat on his bed and scarcely able to open his eyes for more than a second or two. He had deteriorated so much since I'd seen him with the children that I really wanted to know what had happened to him.

Apparently, after my last visit, they had checked his epilepsy treatment and realised that this had been causing the shakes and not the alcohol. However, the treatment he had been given by then had had an enormous effect on him and, apparently, his mind was gone. They tried to tell me that this was the way with alcoholic brain damage and that the medicine had not caused the collapse in his mental faculties. However, they didn't realise that he was such a fighter, and that he had never suffered this kind of treatment before, unlike many of their patients. Few would have suffered cold turkey the number of times that Will had, and survived.

They were by now jumping up and down for his bed as this was an acute and short-stay ward and he had already been in twice as long as normal.

When they realised that he lived on his own, they began muttering about nursing homes, as they were in a bed-blocking situation.

I was absolutely furious. They seemed to want no responsibility for the medical condition they had induced by carrying out the standard treatment without listening to what I had to say, and they were now preparing to write him off.

It was an invidious situation for me to be in, as although, I was his nominated next-of-kin, we were no longer married and I really had no say in the matter.

After all those years, I still knew, better than he did, what was wrong with him and what options were being considered and so I asked if he might be transferred to our local hospital where I could keep an eye on him.

This was obviously the right solution as with long term nursing care he began to improve.

I'm pleased as I can combine a visit to Will with seeing my uncle who is on the same ward with a broken hip. A daily visit there takes only an hour or so and I don't need a granny-sitter. I can also take his washing home before it is minging. Will is still a very sick man, but more cheerful, despite balance problems which means that he can't get out of bed on his own and he still has a degree of confusion mentally and total exhaustion after any effort.

After three months, he is still in hospital with an impaired immune system so that the least thing seems to lay him out flat again. He gets on well with the nurses and the other patients and is, of course, always pleased when I come to visit.

I'm still worried about him, as there seemed to be some other underlying problem in his digestive system. He had earlier had some polyps removed, but the procedure to investigate further was particularly nasty, and although he was mortified one day when he lost control of his bowels, the medical staff didn't think he was strong enough to undertake the journey or the procedure.

Talk about kicking someone when they are down! I am horrified to learn that someone has tried to set Will's flat on fire whilst he is in hospital. They had pushed burning paper through the letterbox. Fortunately, a taxi-driver spotted the flames as he returned home late, and he alerted the fire service. The police found my number in Will's address book and came to let me know. They had boarded it all up, so I have no idea of how much damage had been done. He couldn't go to it when he does come out of hospital until it is all made good.

There didn't seem to be much chance of that happening, as he seems to be getting on quite well, and then, without warning, he is laid flat again with an infection. They were blaming gout, but whatever gave him a high temperature, it had the effect of turning him like a stroke patient again.

The doctors have been talking about nursing homes again, which is worrying, because I'm sure he wouldn't last long there. He would just give up. Anyway, it is not my decision, they will have to speak to him when he is better. There are three patients who have been in for a long time, one is Will, one is showing signs of dementia and the other is a neighbour who had had a stroke and has now caught MRSA. Will is lucky to have avoided that after being in hospital for such a long time.

Ever since the doctors mentioned nursing homes, Will has made a dramatic recovery, not only mentally, but he has also started to go to physiotherapy to improve his walking, and they have got him a monster wheelchair so that he can sit out of bed. He gets desperately tired after his physio, and I have to go and twist the arms of the nurses to let him get back to bed and lie down for a while to recover. The girls and Will's brother came to visit him this weekend. This was the first time that they had seen him since he had been taken to hospital and they were shocked by the change in him, but he is a hundred times better than when he was in Bath. He is so much better than he was

175

then that I am beginning to hope that he will eventually be able to return to his flat. The door will have to be repaired and a shower put in first, and he will need a support package. But I believe he has turned the corner at last.

Christmas is coming and, afterwards, I hope to get away for a real holiday as I'm feeling the strain of caring for my mother and also daily visits to the hospital.

I feel so tired that I scarcely know where to put myself. It has been a real strain to keep everything going, and although I may appear not to worry, I have done more than my fair share.

I started going to an Alpha group run by the Church. They were a super lot of people, very supportive to anyone who was feeling down, and all the participants had their troubles. My experiences were sometimes helpful to others, and the leaders were such caring Christians that it didn't seem to matter if you burst into tears as people frequently did. I decided to start attending services again. I stopped for a long time when I felt embarrassed if I was overcome by emotion and tears during a service. Now, I have realised that it wouldn't matter and that I should put my trust in God. I have been doing an awful lot of praying during the last six months.

I was giving Will a Christmas haircut, using my best dressmaking scissors, when one of my Art Club friends came in to visit someone. They asked if there was no end to my talents. The nurses were not allowed to cut the patient's hair, so he had asked me to do my best, luckily the podiatrist called or that would have been another task. I want to tidy up loose ends before I go on holiday. Mum has been booked into a care home for the time, and my friend has promised to drop by and keep an eye on her.

I got back from a relaxing two weeks cruise and found that things had changed. Will had had his catheters removed and talked himself out of hospital to go home to his flat which, fortunately, had been cleaned up by our cleaner friend. He had been set up with a care package and carers were coming to help him night and morning and he had ordered a supply of frozen foods. The shower was a boon with a seat so there was no balance problem and, fortunately, he had got a mattress protector just in case. His cleaner had agreed to do his washing as well, and all in all, he was reasonably well set up. He would attend the day hospital again for baths and for someone to keep an eye on him, give him physio and a hot mid-day meal. Most of the people at the day hospital were elderly and would nod off after their meal, so Will, who was once again fully in charge mentally, could have a really good chat with the nurses.

I'm so relieved about Will, as my mother had tried so hard to be bright and to do everything right while she had been in the care home, that she is now exhausted and has taken to her bed permanently. At least, it is unlikely now that she will trip and fall, but it is a further step in her decline into old age.

After several months, Will is doing so well that he is down to only an evening visit by carers, and he is back to cooking for himself. He enjoys his supermarket visits and coming to lunch on Sundays, as this is an opportunity to get out of the house. He has finished his period of rehabilitation at the day-hospital, handed back his wheelchair and is fully functioning apart from the fact that his legs are so badly swollen that his balance is poor and he dares not walk out on his own. Now that he is no longer drinking after such a long spell in hospital, he even has the epilepsy under control, and his tablets were reduced when he saw the specialist.

That was until the day that he actually bought another bottle of vodka and attempted to drink it! How stupid can you be?

I found him passed out halfway through the bottle. Needless to say he woke up a sadder and a wiser man. I was incandescent!

"I only bought it to try a glass and see if it would affect me!" he tried to explain. Well, it most certainly did. That was most definitely the last. When he was feeling better and had recovered from the subsequent fit, he swore that he would never be so foolish again. Had he really learned his lesson after all those years?

I certainly hope so. It was such a waste of a good man, a clever engineer, caring husband and father, now reduced to a physical wreck, tired by the least activity and unable to enjoy the things that had once given him so much pleasure, like walking in the country, gardening and DIY. No longer could he really enjoy the company of his family. It has been a waste of my life too in false hopes and then the despair of watching him decline. It wasted the young lives of his daughters who didn't have a good father to rely on when they needed him. He has wasted some of the time he might have spent with his grandchildren, and the opportunity of sharing with them the country lore they all would have enjoyed. All the fun things in life had been replaced by worry, concern and mistrust.

I still have some hopes for the future, but it is in shades of grey rather than the rainbow.

Was this all there was?'

Now she has gone and left him alone
Lonely and broken in health.
He survived her grim touch
Lay 'twixt death and life
'Til he chose to live
With the help of his wife
His friend who is there for him still.
Through the years so much waste
So few joys, so much ill
'Til his world is shrunk down to one room
Too late to do all the things we had planned
But at least he returned from his doom.

Poem Written in 2003

Epilogue

It would have been good to report that from then on he had been able to stay on the straight and narrow, but he did try, most of the time. Fortunately, the corner shop off-licence closed down so it was more difficult for him to obtain supplies. He continued to go to the supermarket with Liz and to go for Sunday lunch, however there came a great change in her life.

With her mother confined to bed and gardening on a hill, it was too much in her old house and she moved to occupy her aunt's bungalow when her aunt went into a care home. By the time it had been modified to suit her needs, Liz's mother was fast heading into a world of her own, her hearing difficulties exacerbating dementia and delusions. In the bungalow, Liz was always on hand to calm her when wild animals came in through the windows, or when her long dead relatives and friends came to visit.

"It is as if she has her very own video programme which, of course, I cannot share and she gets most upset," explained Liz to her friends.

Caring for her mother was a full time job, but she still managed to have all the grandchildren to stay at holiday times, as Jane too had had to divorce her husband and become a single mother. Liz was pulled three ways and was enormously glad of the help granny-sitting offered by her friends, and at times, also for paid help too.

Will would have liked to be able to offer his help as well, but her mother was a bit scared of him after all these years, and he still couldn't be fully trusted to be reliable enough. Liz was pleased to be able to share her worries with him, but his health was too bad for him to be able to give her practical help.

He still came up for Sunday lunch and usually provided the joint ready cooked, as Liz didn't have a proper oven. Will even bought a scooter so that he could travel up under his own steam. He had enjoyed the rides when they made a trip to the local arboretum and hired a scooter there so he thought he would have his own.

Being able to get out alone was not necessarily a good move as it opened the way to temptation at the local supermarket. He made sure he had recovered by the weekend, though, as he didn't want stoppage of visiting rights. Liz had really frightened him.

Liz got ill with all the stress, and her friend threatened to ring up and get a proper social service assessment so she made the contact herself and was able to get carers several times a week to get a break. She had developed gastric problems and needed medical treatment. Will was concerned but unable to help.

So things continued for a year or so during which a whole menagerie had been attacking the front window, and Liz heard her mother swear as never before! She managed to get away on holiday a couple of times when it became too much, and discovered that the team of carers could manage without her, briefly. She hadn't known before that you could employ live-in carers for a couple of weeks at a time to give her respite.

At Christmas, Will was beginning to have problems with incontinence and was terribly embarrassed. Urinary incontinence was one thing and could be handled. But the other! Liz was forever ferrying pads and pants for her mother or for Will. It was just one of those things. So long as people didn't think they were for her!

Will became reluctant to go out at all, and was beginning to feel too weak to sit upon his scooter. Liz got the doctor to prescribe some pills. It was Will's usual doctor, who seemed reluctant to refer him to find out what was really the matter. Once an alcoholic, everything became blamed upon the drink, even though he wasn't fit to get any, and neither Liz nor his cleaner would dream of it. They had enough of a job with him already.

After five months, Liz lost her patience and really jumped up and down until the doctor made a referral.

When he got to hospital, he was scarcely able to sit up, let alone stand and Liz made sure that she had some nightwear and toiletries in the car.

He was admitted for multiple tests to find out what was happening to him. He looked really terrible again and Liz called his brother down to see him. Finally, but finally, they decided that his pancreas had packed up and he had really bad diabetes. That would account for the incontinence, but the delay in getting treatment meant that he could no longer walk and needed to be shipped out to a nursing home.

The nearest available place was a 30 mile round trip from home, and although the staff were very good, it was impossible for Liz to get there very often as her mother needed her care.

Once again, Will rallied. He taught himself to walk again, despite the prognosis, and in six months was fit enough to be reclassified for residential care and transferred to the new care home that had been built where the local hospital had been. He had had to agree to give up his flat even after it had all been redecorated for him, and he knew that his only option was now residential care – at ruinous expense. He was taking more than 30 tablets a day and before long had to have insulin as well.

Fully in control of his mental faculties again, he was scathing of the management of the home – it wouldn't have done for the Navy – but got on well with the nursing staff and the few residents who were not suffering from dementia. For him, it was like being condemned to prison and his only escape was when Liz arranged to take him home for Sunday lunch, although, he had to be back for tea and his next round of tablets.

He had been there for two years before Liz's mother took a turn for the worse and died at the age of 103, the oldest resident in the town. She had even outlasted some of Liz's friends who used to granny-sit for her.

Will was determined to attend her funeral, for he had always thought a lot of her and wanted to be there for the family. He came out for the day with a bin liner full of the tablets that were prescribed in his name and Ann, the nurse, promised to give him the right doses.

Liz was devastated by her loss and planned a long trip to Australia to have something to focus upon…

Six months later, she set out and received a family welcome from Will's sister whom she hadn't seen for 40 years. Apparently, she was the only one who had corresponded all this time and sent her all the news about her brothers. Will was quietly pleased when he heard about this.

On her return, Liz was able to visit the families of her daughters and grandchildren more often and also made a point of visiting Will several times a week and telephoning nightly. So he was kept in touch with the news of the family and particularly the grandchildren who were growing up fast. He was inordinately proud of them all.

Finally, the following Christmas, Will was pleased to tell Liz that he had got rid of the PTSD, that he had been suffering from since the Falklands War, and he was more contented in himself.

He still considered himself confined to a prison, and an expensive one at that for almost all his savings had been used up on his care and so too was all his pension so that he had nothing to be able to buy things for his family if he wanted to.

Two months later, the examination that he had been too ill to undertake all those years earlier was rescheduled. (They had probably lost track of him and thought that he had not survived.) Sadly, this showed that the polyp they had been unable to remove earlier had turned cancerous.

It was inoperable and radiotherapy treatment left him unable to leave his bedroom and take part in the normal meals in the care home. The old ladies, who had adopted him as their 'toy-boy' when he took care of their interests, were without their champion. They were most upset.

Finally, however, Will was able to appreciate his surroundings and the care that the staff provided him when help was really needed.

He spent the rest of the year very appreciative of what they did for him.

***

When he died, the following Christmas, he left a hole in several hearts, not least in Liz's.

She had been away on holiday in December and during that time he had gone downhill rapidly, but fortunately had managed to heal his relationship with his daughters by long telephone conversations. When Liz saw him again, she knew it would not be long and on the Sunday he was visited by his daughters and eldest grand-daughter who had come to say goodbye. On Christmas Eve, he was taken into hospital where he died on Boxing Day.

It was hard for Liz having to agree with the hospital doctor that DNR was the appropriate path and harder still realising that because they were divorced, she was unable to register his death. Fortunately their younger daughter, who was also there at the critical time, could.

Happily he had been totally reconciled with all his family in his last days and many tears were shed at his funeral.

***

Two months later, Liz was on a cruise that she had booked months earlier.

A psychic healer, whom Liz met on her travels, gave her a message. She said that she had been in contact with someone who wanted to give her this message. She told Liz that Will was still watching over her and wanted her to know that he was sorry for everything and that he could now walk again. The following day, the psychic presented Liz with three roses that Will had asked her to buy for "his girls".

That was good for a few more tears. Liz missed him more than she ever realised was possible even though their lives had been together for 50 years.

***

Will's ashes were scattered on his birthday on the waters of the Solent, at a beach where he used to walk his dogs.

As she did this last service for him and said a final farewell, the rainy skies lifted and a path of golden sunlight led across the water to Liz.

She turned, with her younger daughter and two grandsons, and before them they saw a perfect rainbow curved over the beach huts.

"I think he was pleased," she said, and they all burst into tears.

The Rainbow

Wander o'er the pebbles
All along the shore
Memories are returning
Happy days and more.

Along the beach, next to the sea
The little waves bring you closer to me.
You went away to distant lands
The sea our link, the sea and sands.

Wander o'er the pebbles
All along the shore
Memories are returning.
Happy days and more.

I used to wonder, "Where are you now?"
As I walked on my side when time would allow.
"Are you awake, can you see the ocean?
"Or are you asleep, rocked by its motion?"

Wander o'er the pebbles
All along the shore
Memories are returning
Happy days and more.

Sundays were bad, when families gather
And I walked on my side, whatever the weather.
The falling rain hides tears of pain.
Wind makes my eyes to cry.
The sunshine bright makes me squint in the light
And then my face is dry.

You walked the dogs along the shore.
Sniff at the tide-line, run, splash some more.
Oh how they smelled after that run!
Tongues flopping out, hot in the sun.

Wander o'er the pebbles
All along the shore
Memories are returning
Happy days and more.

Dogs, man and sea, all linked in my mind.
The girls and me, always behind.
Those times are past, time has moved on
The dogs and the man, now they are gone.

The falling rain hides tears of pain.
Wind makes my eyes to cry.
The sunshine bright makes me squint in the light
And then my face is dry.

We said farewell down there on the shore.
You floated away. We could do no more.

But as we watched, the sun came through
A golden path 'twixt me and you.
We turned. A rainbow shining there
A symbol that we all can share

That in the times of deepest woe.
When finally you must let go.
'Tis not the end of me and you.
God's promise holds forever true.

Wander o'er the pebbles
All along the shore
Memories are returning
Happy days and more

The falling rain hides tears of pain
Wind makes my eyes to cry
The sunshine bright, makes me squint in the light
And soon my face is dry.

Poem Written in 2013

Postscript

This story which started out as a lament has ended up as a story of enduring love, of many starts, of many failures, of many hurts, but of continuing hope.

I hope that it will bring some comfort to those who are still dealing with the cruel mistress in the glass and with the incubus in the corner, surrounded by its dark cloud.

For those who are dogged by depression for whatever reason, I beg of you to talk to someone who may be able to understand.

Jill Stephens